100 YEARS OF STYLE

BY DECADE
& DESIGNER

VOLUME 4

TWENTIETH CENTURY
FASHION DESIGNERS
G–M

This edition copyright 2001 by Chelsea House Publishers, a subsidiary
of Haights Cross Communications. Printed and bound in Dubai.

First printing

1 3 5 7 9 8 6 4 2

The Chelsea House World Wide Web address is
http://www.chelseahouse.com

Library of Congress Cataloging-in-Publication Data applied for

ISBN 0 7910 6195 7 Fashion Designers G–M (this edition)

0 7910 6192 2 Fashions 1900–1949
0 7910 6193 0 Fashions 1950–1999
0 7910 6194 9 Fashion Designers A–F
0 7910 6196 5 Fashion Designers N–Z
0 7910 6191 4 (set)

Produced by Carlton Books
20 Mortimer Street
London W1N 7RD

Text and Design copyright © Carlton Books Limited 1999/2000

Photographs copyright © 1999 Condé Nast Publications Limited

Previous page: Sleek tailoring with seams precisely positioned
for maximum fit and flare effect: Muir's perfect suit, 1986.

Opposite: John Galliano shows his incurably romantic streak
in his lilac silk crinoline skirt and pale blue jacket
trimmed with blue swansdown.

Overleaf: Savile Row-trained
McQueen uses a blend of angles,
curves and subtle colour to make suits
that are anything but straight, 1998.

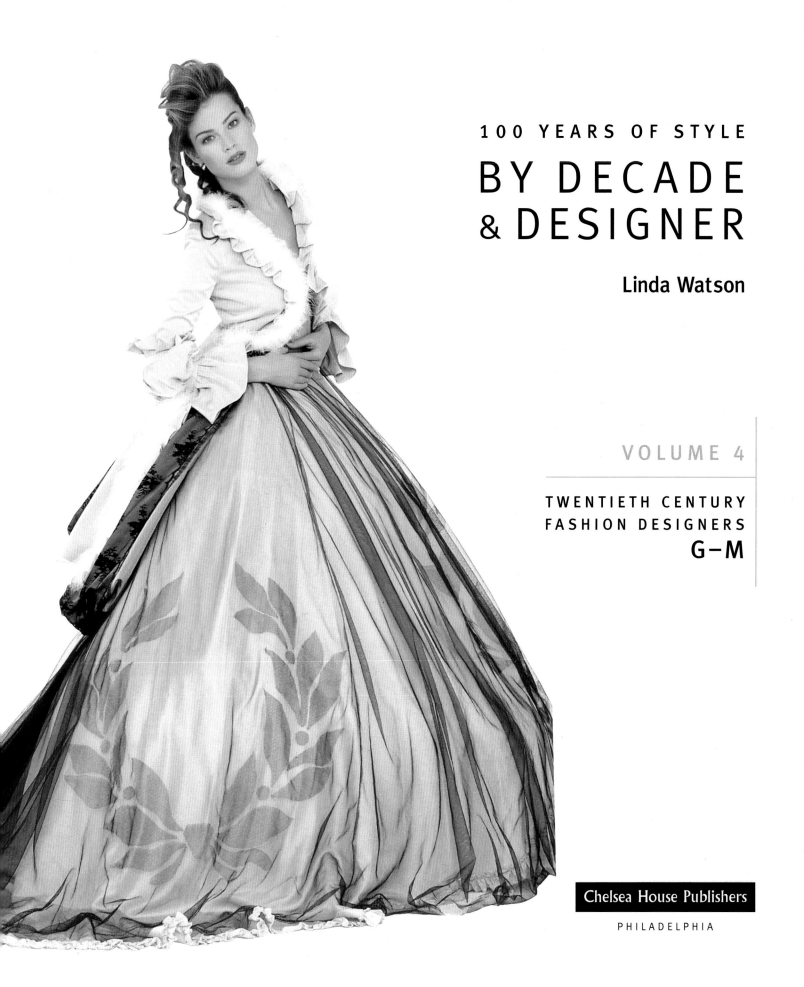

100 YEARS OF STYLE

BY DECADE
& DESIGNER

Linda Watson

VOLUME 4

TWENTIETH CENTURY
FASHION DESIGNERS
G–M

Chelsea House Publishers

PHILADELPHIA

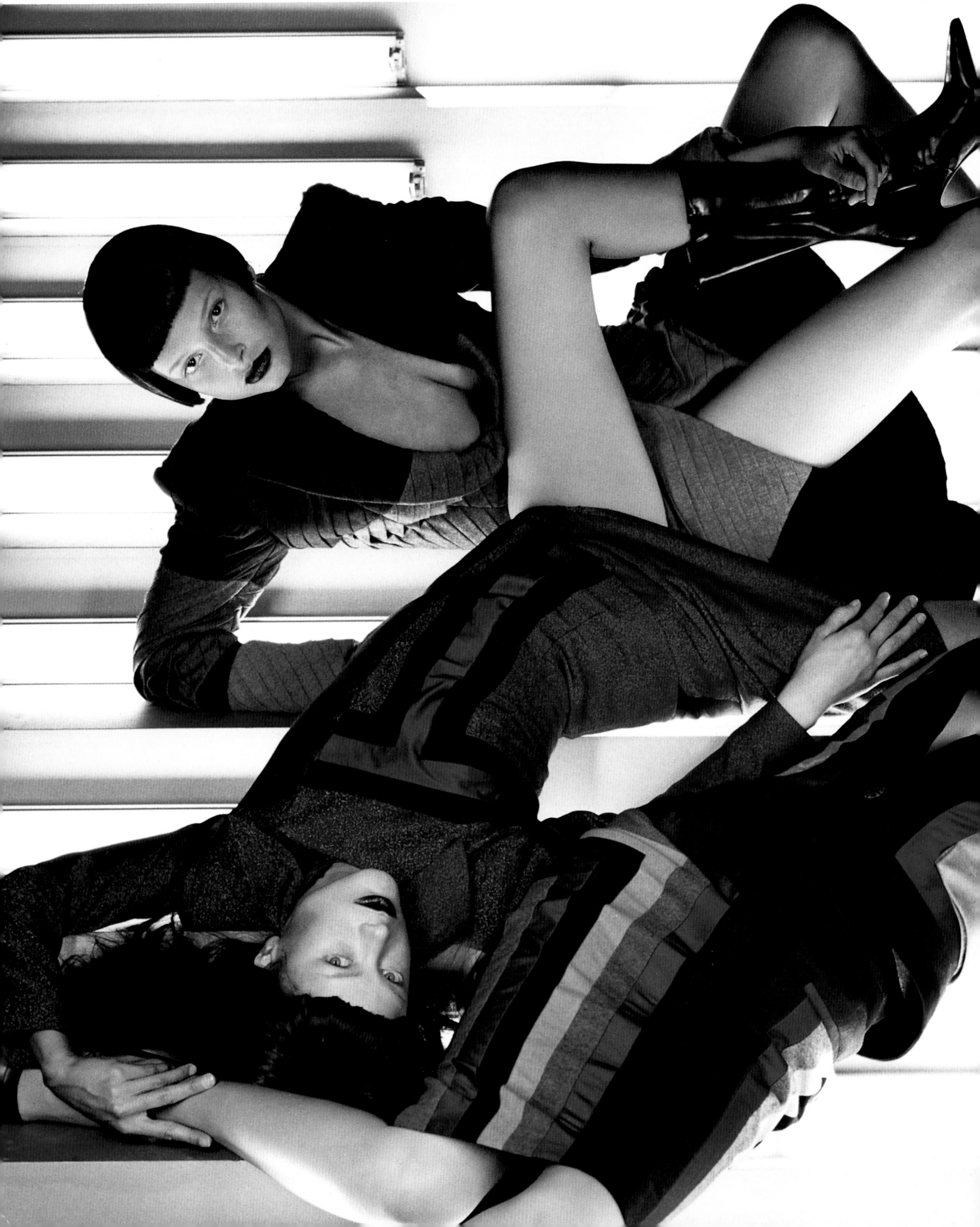

contents

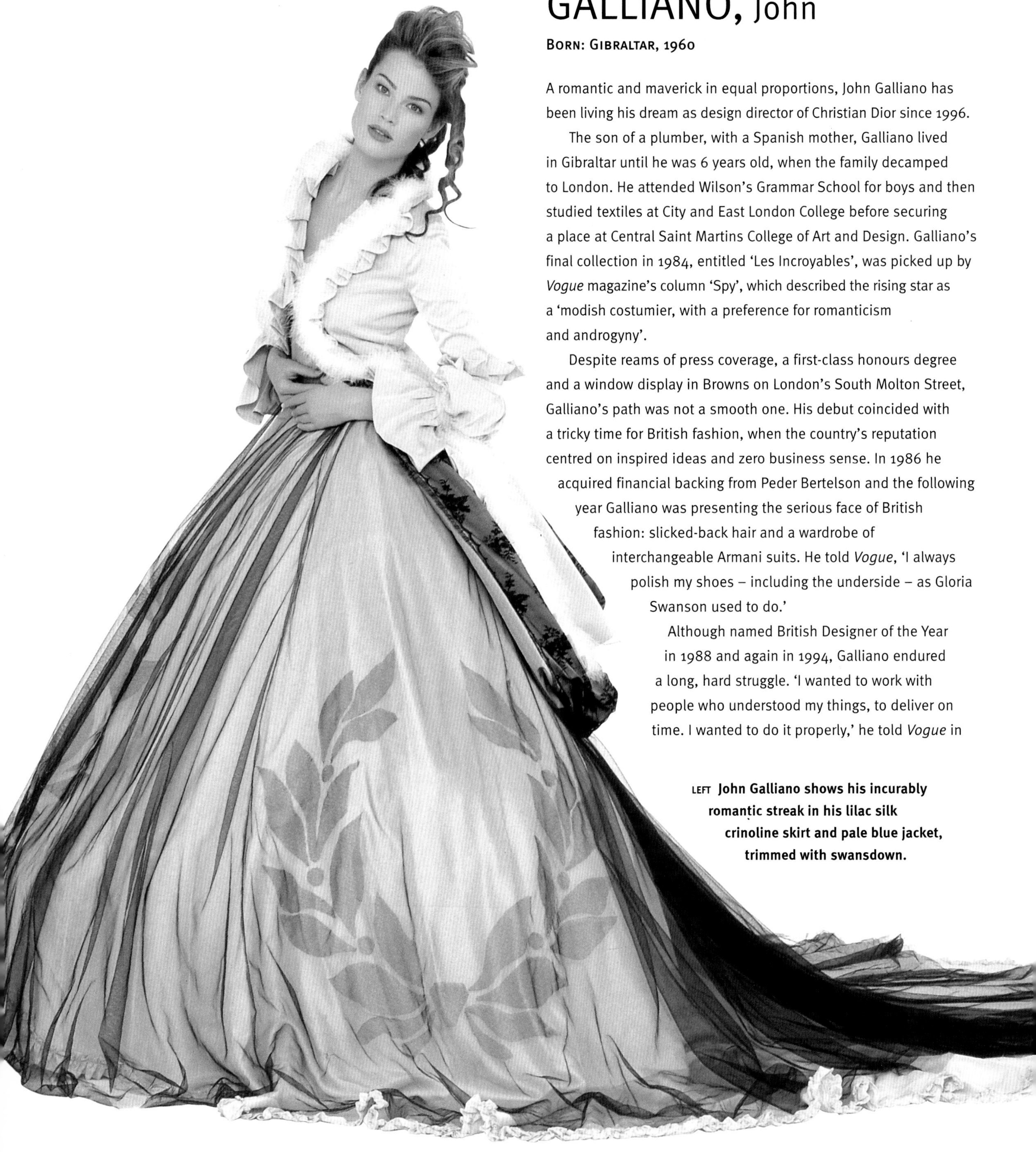

GALLIANO, John

BORN: GIBRALTAR, 1960

A romantic and maverick in equal proportions, John Galliano has been living his dream as design director of Christian Dior since 1996.

The son of a plumber, with a Spanish mother, Galliano lived in Gibraltar until he was 6 years old, when the family decamped to London. He attended Wilson's Grammar School for boys and then studied textiles at City and East London College before securing a place at Central Saint Martins College of Art and Design. Galliano's final collection in 1984, entitled 'Les Incroyables', was picked up by *Vogue* magazine's column 'Spy', which described the rising star as a 'modish costumier, with a preference for romanticism and androgyny'.

Despite reams of press coverage, a first-class honours degree and a window display in Browns on London's South Molton Street, Galliano's path was not a smooth one. His debut coincided with a tricky time for British fashion, when the country's reputation centred on inspired ideas and zero business sense. In 1986 he acquired financial backing from Peder Bertelson and the following year Galliano was presenting the serious face of British fashion: slicked-back hair and a wardrobe of interchangeable Armani suits. He told *Vogue*, 'I always polish my shoes – including the underside – as Gloria Swanson used to do.'

Although named British Designer of the Year in 1988 and again in 1994, Galliano endured a long, hard struggle. 'I wanted to work with people who understood my things, to deliver on time. I wanted to do it properly,' he told *Vogue* in

LEFT John Galliano shows his incurably romantic streak in his lilac silk crinoline skirt and pale blue jacket, trimmed with swansdown.

1988. International success was elusive, backers came and went, and Galliano often produced collections while sleeping on friends' floors. When financial constraints dictated a new direction, Galliano brought out a cheaper line – Galliano's Girl in 1991, followed by Galliano Genes. Despite his aptitude for diffusion lines, he remained a couturier at heart, often fingering toiles by Balenciaga and Charles James in the vaults of London's Victoria and Albert Museum.

Galliano's pursuit of recognition was relentless. He moved to Paris in 1994, and two years later made a resounding impression with an impeccable collection inspired by the opera *Madame Butterfly*. In one fell swoop, Galliano underlined the purity and modernity of the kimono.

After months of feverish speculation, on 11 July 1995, Galliano was appointed the successor to Hubert de Givenchy – and made history as the first British designer to be appointed head of an established French house. On 14 October 1996 John Galliano was appointed design director of Christian Dior, his debut unveiled on 20 January 1997.

Galliano is first and foremost a romantic. He is also a historian, an explorer, and a person who is unashamedly in love with fabric and form. Some say his heart rules his head. No one questions his talent. Galliano remains a fabulously inventive designer with a healthy respect for the house built by the legendary Christian Dior.

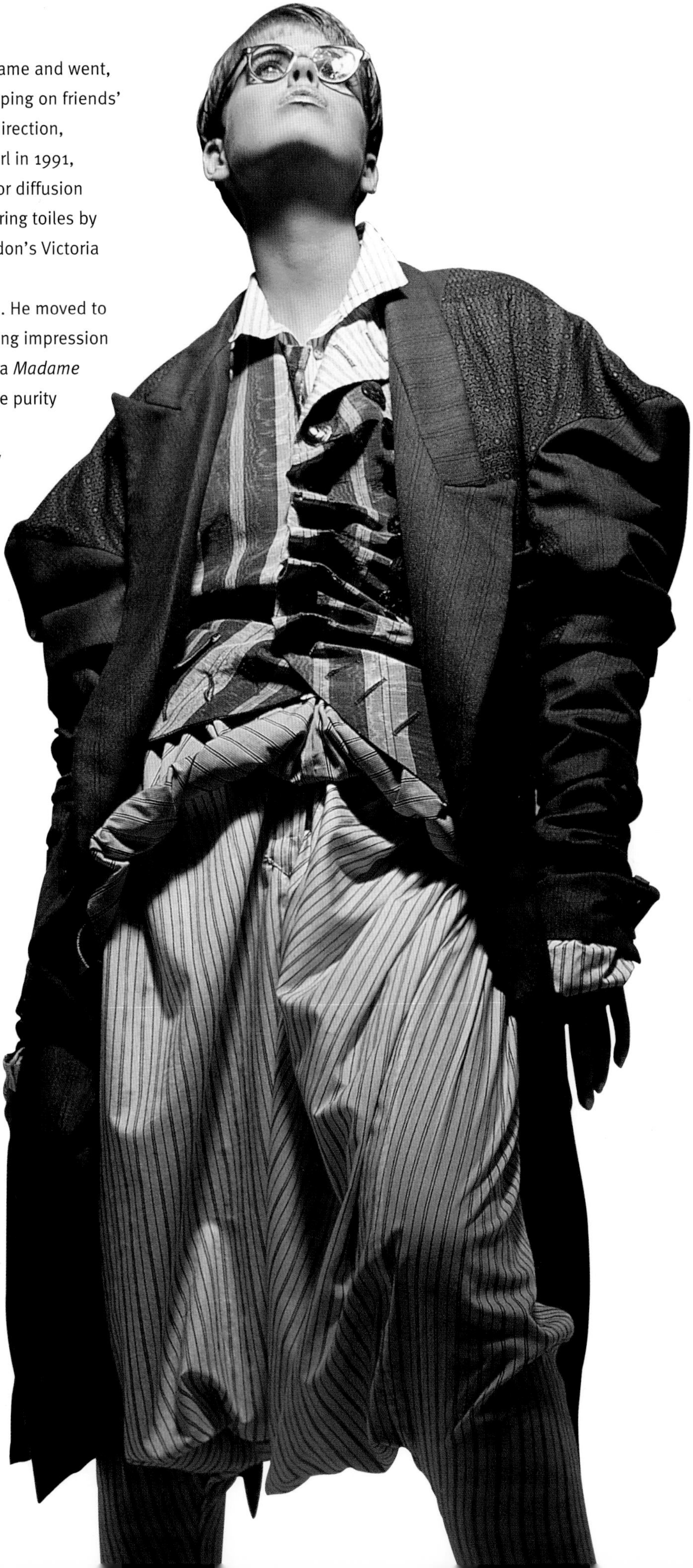

RIGHT 'First smash your specs': Galliano's radical ensemble of 1985 with 'rolluppable' back, sleeves to the knees and mismatched buttoning.

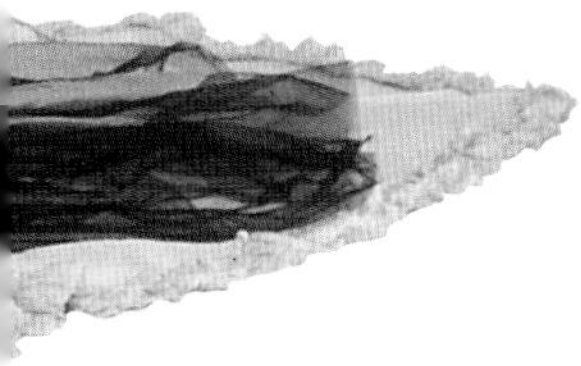

GAULTIER, Jean Paul

BORN: ARCUEIL, FRANCE, 1952

The description '*enfant terrible*' has followed Jean Paul Gaultier (the son of two accountants) around for over 20 years. Now nudging 50 years old, Gaultier does 60 daily press-ups and sports cropped peroxide-blond hair.

Gaultier's career commenced on his eighteenth birthday when he was employed as a sketcher at Pierre Cardin. A year later he moved to Esterel, then to Jean Patou, where he worked for two years – first with Michael Gomez, then Angelo Tarlazzi – before returning to Cardin, based in the fashion backwater of Manila in the Philippines. Gaultier returned to Paris in 1976 and began making electronic jewellery with his partner, Francis Menuge, and in 1978 presented his first fashion collection without success. 'I was a joke for three years,' he told the *Sunday Express* in 1987, 'And in France to be a joke is not funny.' He hit his stride in the mid-1980s, generating reams of newspaper copy with his catwalk escapades, conical corsetry and skirts for men. The latter, he claimed at the time, resulted in sales of 3,000 skirts worldwide. *Vogue* described an early collection as 'a motley fusion of punk pilferings, slattern sophistication and B-movie anecdotes'. His finest hour was dressing Madonna in a mix of satin corsetry and black bondage for her Blonde Ambition tour of 1990.

No one could accuse Gaultier of being a one-trick pony. He successfully produces both mens- and womenswear, diffusion and couture. Gaultier has run the gamut from fetishistic fabrics – rubber and PVC – to conventional wools and cotton/Lycra. His first fur collection was unveiled in 1998. He has worked several times with choreographer Régine Chopinot, dressed countless pop stars and even released his own album of house music, *How to do that?*, with Tony Mansfield, in 1989. His cinematic costume credits include *City of the Lost Children* (1995) by Caro and Jeunet, Luc Besson's *The Fifth Element* (1997) and, the one which was probably most suited to his style, Peter Greenaway's 1989 celebration of decadence, *The Cook, the Thief, his Wife and her Lover*. Gaultier's autobiography, *A Nous Deux la Mode*, published in 1990, was suitably kitsch in content and cover, with Gaultier posing in a nautical striped T- shirt, surrounded by flowers. In 1999 he was the first French fashion designer to go on-line.

A self-confessed Anglophile, who is more likely to be found rummaging in Camden market than admiring historical exhibits, Gaultier co-hosted *Eurotrash*, a saucy tabloid television show, during the 1990s. He appeared weekly, invariably wearing a kilt and a wide grin, and played up his French accent for all it was worth.

In 1997 Gaultier's first couture collection revealed a host of hidden attributes – restraint for one – and received favourable reviews. In one of his earliest *Vogue* appearances he said, 'My affinities are with the young and unorthodox, so I create costumes that break rules, go over the top if you like ...' Irony is still his speciality. Long may his quirkiness continue.

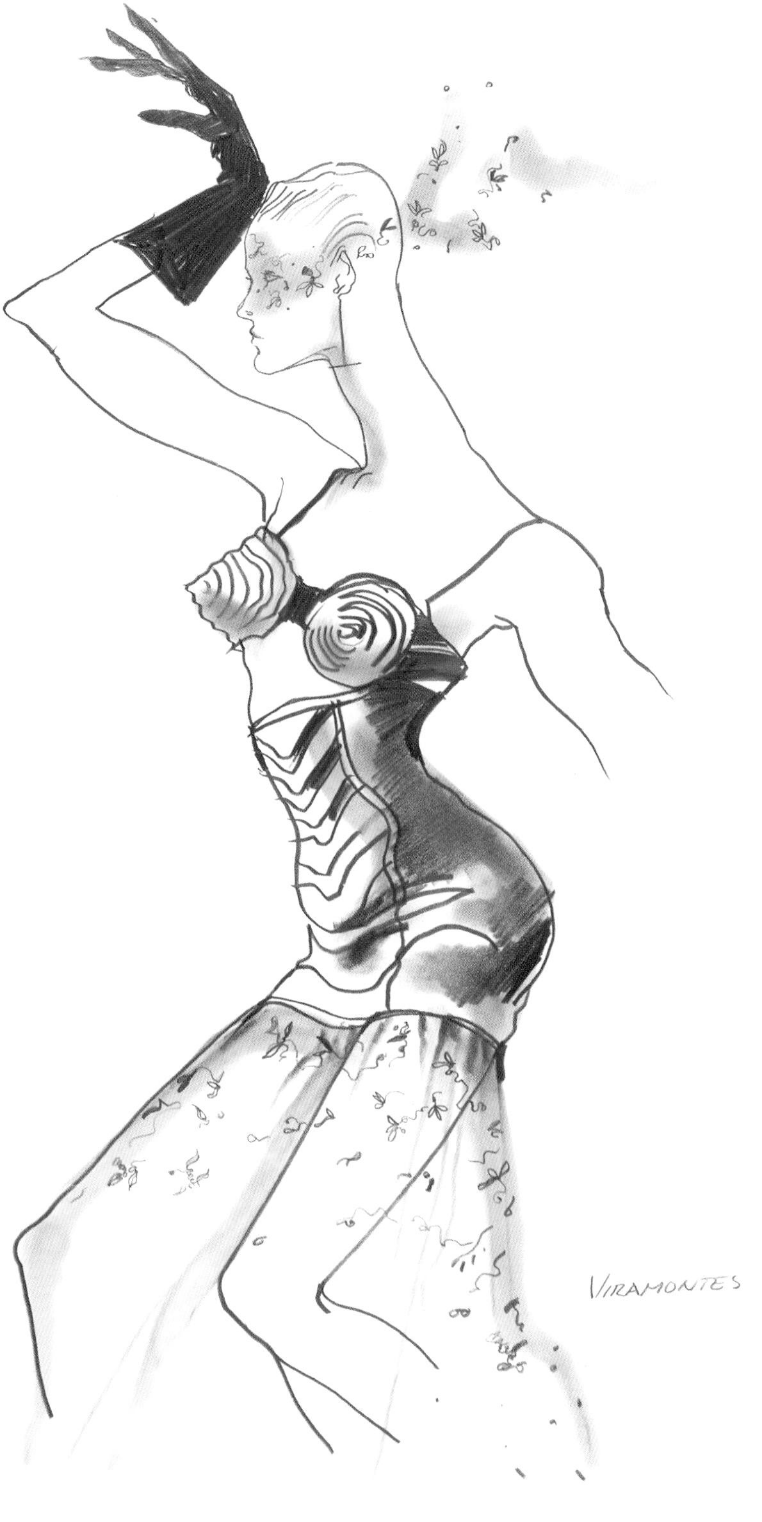
VIRAMONTES

ABOVE Gaultier's infamous conical corset of 1983. The cups became more elongated and outrageous as the decade progressed.

OPPOSITE The subdued side of Gaultier: flounced chiffon petticoats, metallic silk, garlands of flowers and 1950s' quiffs, 1995.

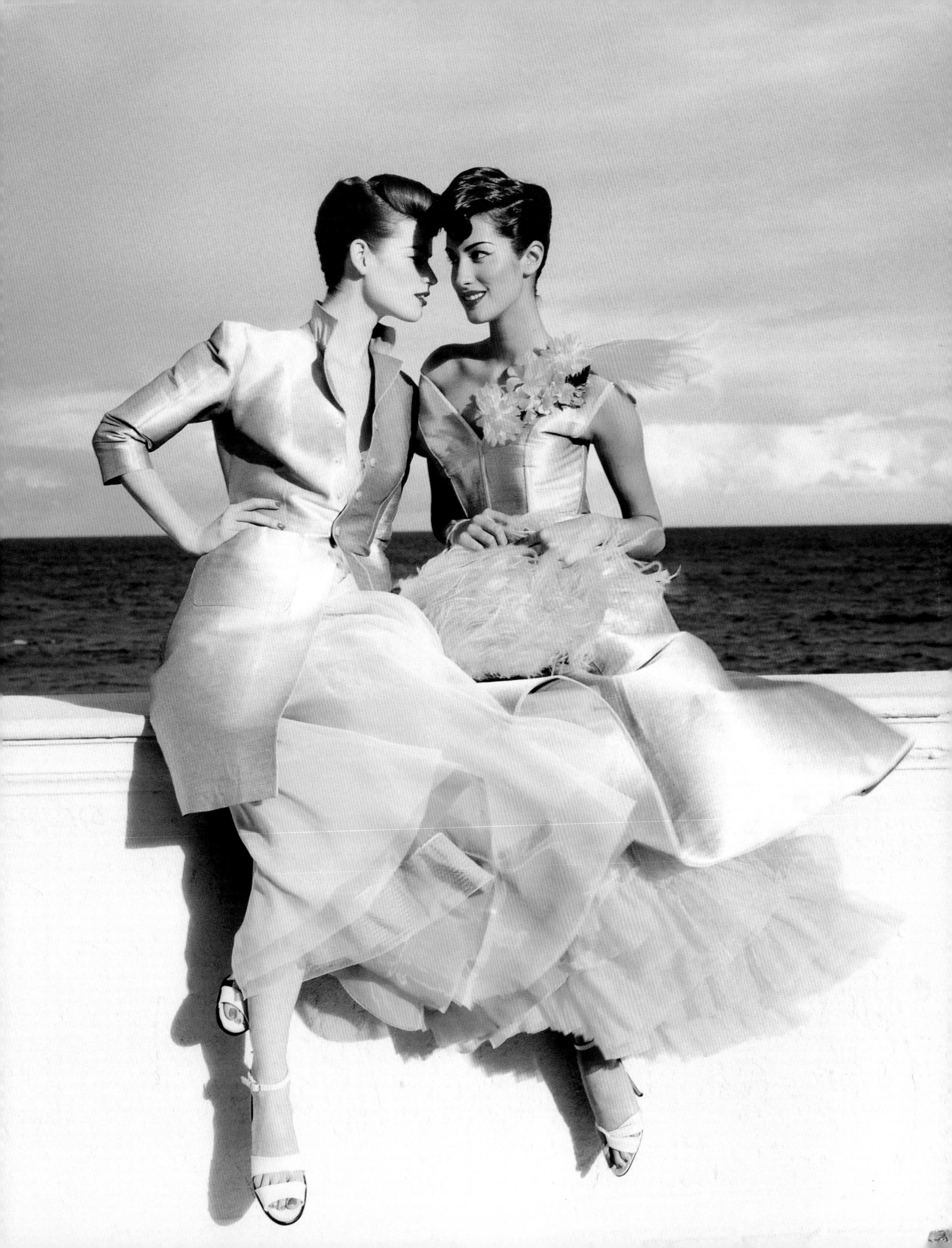

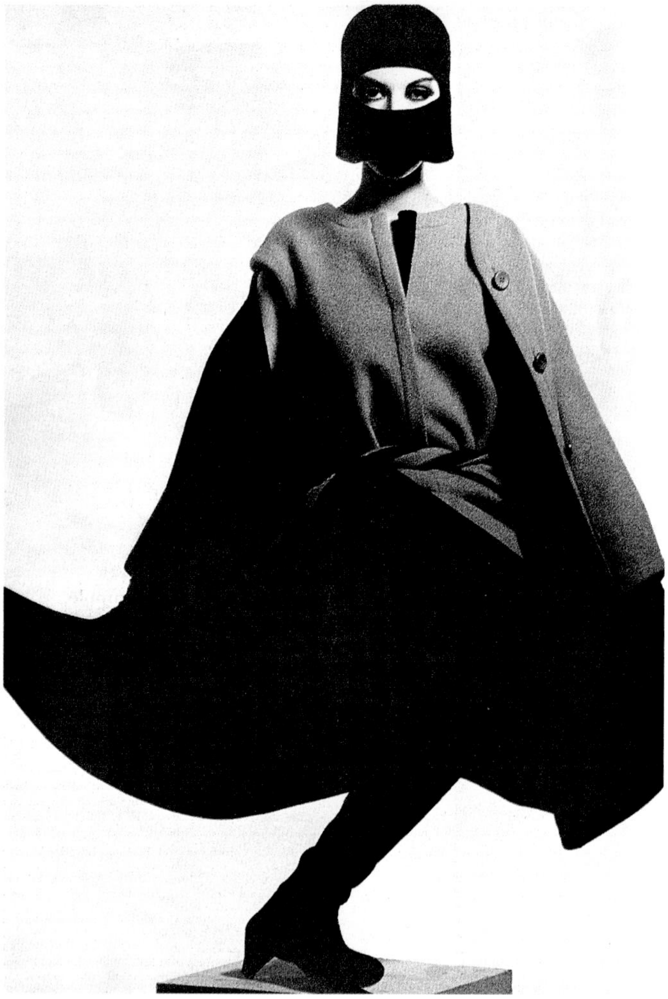

LEFT America's foremost modernist, Rudi Gernreich, creating waves from his Californian studio with helmet, cape coat, and 'Brave New World', 1964.

GERNREICH, Rudi

BORN: VIENNA, AUSTRIA, 1922
DIED: LOS ANGELES, CALIFORNIA, USA, 1985

The dancer turned designer, who many regard as America's answer to Pierre Cardin, Rudi Gernreich was a 1960s' experimentalist, most famous for the topless swimsuit, which he launched in 1964.

Gernreich's career followed a natural path. He studied at Los Angles City College, later becoming a dancer and costume designer with the Lester Horton Dance Company. He designed freelance for a variety of markets, including swimwear, shoes and knitwear before opening his own showroom on Seventh Avenue in New York, which straddled two lines of knitwear and experimental ideas.

It was Gernreich's infamous breast-exposing swimsuit that spread his notoriety and secured his place in fashion history. Like the French futurists of the 1960s, Gernreich was experimenting with plastics and vinyl fabrics, exploring the idea of unisex clothes and inventions with self-explanatory titles: namely the No-Bra Bra and Pubikini. His model and muse Peggy Moffitt, who modelled the topless swimsuit, had a suitably startling look which dovetailed with Gernreich's vision of the future.

GHOST

FOUNDED BY TANYA SARNE IN 1984

Languid lines, flowing shapes and the absence of any sharp edges are the signatures of the Ghost label. Founded by Tanya Sarne, Ghost is a commercial and design success because it fulfils the criteria of modern design for comfort and fluidity by using practical fabrics which rarely crease and adapt to varying shapes and sizes. Launched in the era of the outrageously large shoulder pad, Ghost is a collection with mass appeal – a worldwide bestseller, with 80 per cent of its custom divided between the USA, Japan, Europe, Australia and the Middle East. The company was awarded the British Apparel Export Award in 1992. In 1999 Ghost decided to swap London Fashion Week for a show in New York.

GIBB, Bill

BORN: FRASERBURGH, SCOTLAND, 1943
DIED: LONDON, ENGLAND, 1988

The creator of some of the century's most mind-blowing dresses, Bill Gibb's celtic sensibility, love of craftsmanship and extraordinary colour sense made him a star in the truest sense of the word. 'It would be hard to imagine anyone less pompous than Bill Gibb,' said *Vogue* in 1977 on the eve of his ten-year retrospective at the Albert Hall in London. 'He wears a broad smile, a long floppy scarf and strange knit bobble hat. Who else would have laughed when Elizabeth Taylor wore one of his dresses back to front on television?'

Son of a New Pisligo farmer, Gibb switched from farming to fashion with the greatest of ease. He studied at the Royal College of Art in London in 1966, but left to do his own thing after just a year. Gibb then joined the shop Baccarat as a freelance designer, later working in collaboration with knitwear designer, Kaffe Fassett. A typical Bill Gibb creation had a simple shape and fantastical surface – a gorgeous entity which employed his team of knitters, weavers, embroiderers and printers. At the height of his career, Gibb's clients included Eartha Kitt, Tina Chow, Twiggy and the Empress of Iran. 'Everywhere I move I take four things with me,'

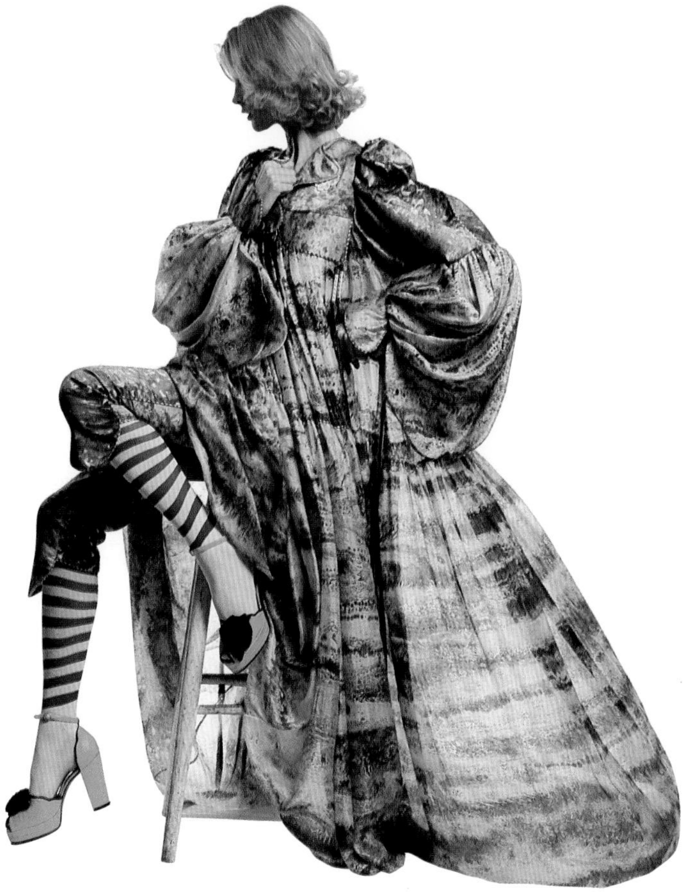

LEFT **Bill Gibb, 1970, blending the finest crafts on the planet: embroidered suede, ribbons, slashed sleeves, satin, and two prints together.**

BELOW **Gigli's sweeping wraparound coat of many colours was 'worn by angelic models'. An overnight sensation of winter, 1989.**

he said, 'two chemist chests, a 1930s' porcelain head, and my collection of bees.' Bill Gibb, sensitive, original and self-effacing, was most suited to a period which appreciated craft and worshipped surface texture. His dresses – perfect expressions of hippiedom – were sadly out of sync with the late 1970s, while his talent was probably best summed up by Beatrix Miller, former editor of British *Vogue*, who commented in his obituary in 1988. 'Perhaps he never found his métier, and it is cruel that fashion decreed he never would. Theatre, ballet, opera might have given him the scope he needed.'

GIGLI, Romeo

BORN: CASTELBOLOGNESE, ITALY, 1949

'When I'm working on a collection I'm not thinking,' said Romeo Gigli of his divine inspiration in 1989, 'it's a spontaneous, chemical thing.'

Both Gigli's father and grandfather were antiquarian book dealers and he spent his childhood surrounded by his father's collection of 20,000 books from the fifteenth and sixteenth centuries. Gigli originally trained as an architect and spent four years living on the Balearic island of Ibiza before moving to Milan. In 1972 the owner of a store in Bologna asked Gigli to design. He moved to New York in 1978 and designed a collection for Piero Dimitri.

With sloping shoulders, beautiful colours, opulent fabrics and flat pumps, Gigli reintroduced the Renaissance woman just at the point when big shoulders were beginning to fall out of favour.

Gigli set up his own label in 1983, but it was not until his fourth season, in March 1986 – following a show of elongated knitwear and languid lines – that he was heralded 'a quiet new talent' by *The New York Times*. In March 1989 Gigli decided to show in Paris for the first time. Backed by Zamasport, his autumn/winter Byzantine collection was rapturously received by the international buyers. He launched the perfume, Romeo, later that year and rode the crest of rave reviews. A diffusion line and G Gigli was on the horizon, but behind the scenes Gigli was facing a business fracas involving two former business partners. This dispute did not reach a settlement until May 1991, when Gigli regained control.

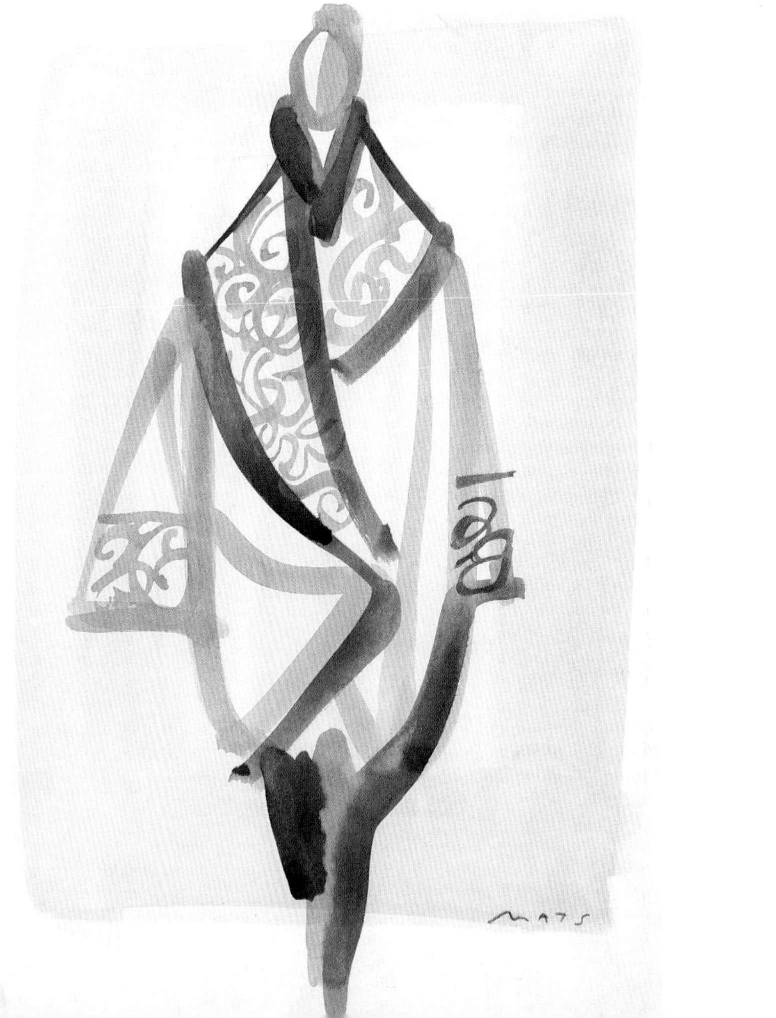

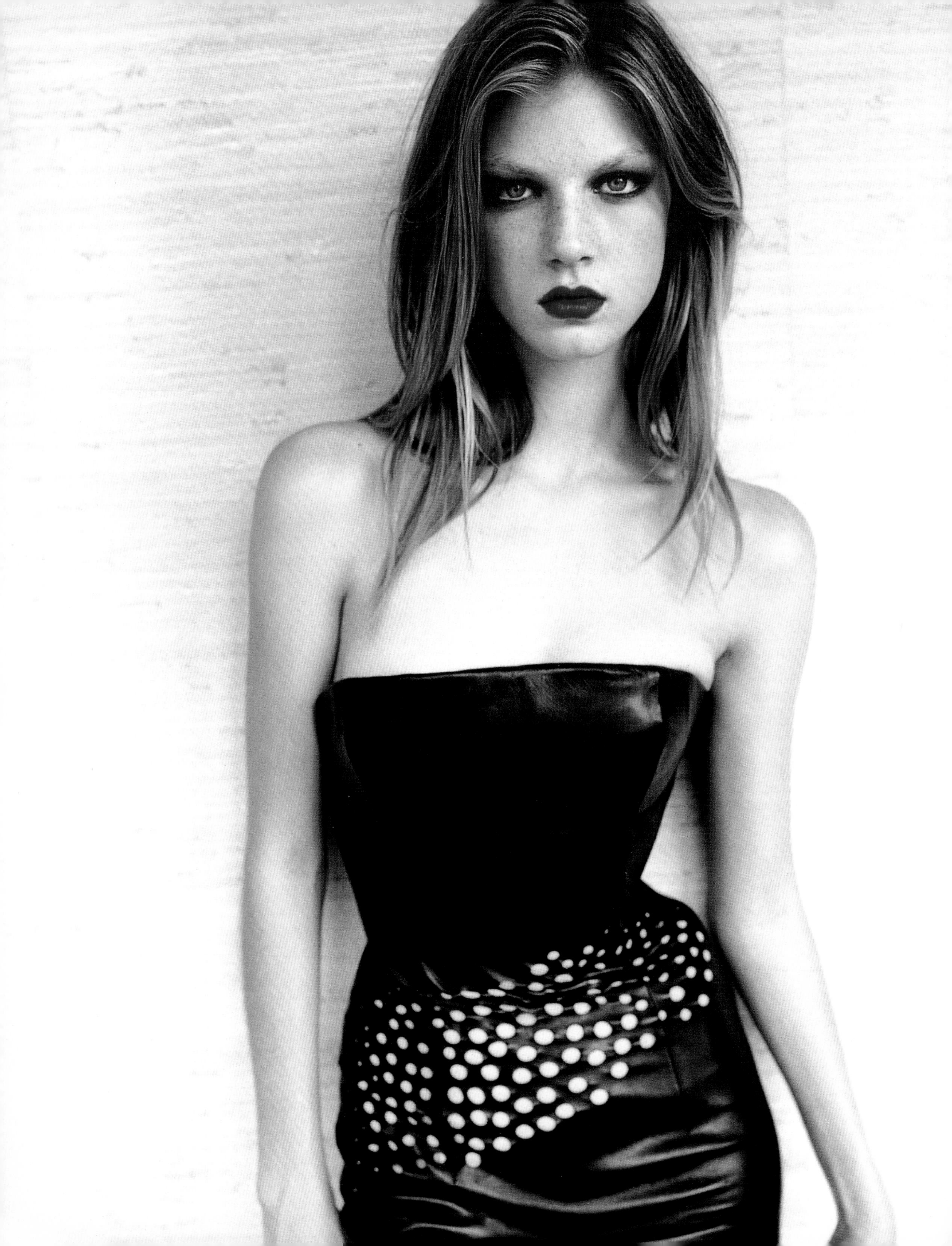

GIVENCHY, Hubert de

Born: Beauvais, France, 1927

Hubert de Givenchy's quest for perfection was a direct consequence of his friendship with Cristobal Balenciaga. For 40 years he wore his mentor's white coat at the end of each show. 'Monsieur Balenciaga gave it to me,' he told *Vogue* in 1991. 'It is like a talisman, a protection, a second skin.' Givenchy's 1952 philosophy on economy was years ahead of its time: 'All a woman needs to be chic are a raincoat, two suits, a pair of trousers and a cashmere sweater.' His own suits are made by Huntsman of Savile Row, London.

Having studied at College Félix Faure in Beauvais and then at the École Nationale Supérieure des Beaux Arts in Paris, Givenchy worked with Jacques Fath, Robert Piguet, Lucien Lelong and at Elsa Schiaparelli before opening his own house on 2 February 1952 on the rue Alfred de Vigny at the age of 25. *Vogue* described him as, 'One of the most newsworthy happenings this spring. The applause at his premiere was loud, unqualified, and long.' First-day sales totalled seven million francs.

By 1963 Balenciaga and Givenchy were being talked about in the same breath. 'Between them, Balenciaga and Givenchy innovate and predict, with an equal profundity of perfection and clear-sighted boldness that needs no excessive extravagance to be understood,' wrote *Vogue*. A decade later, Givenchy was enjoying the fruits of his labour; *Vogue* described his impeccable apartment, hung with a Picasso: 'The setting is superb but then so is Givenchy. The beautiful blue Miró hangs high like a patch of rippling June sky above a drawing room that is so luxe, so polished, so civilised, so burnished, that it practically turns over and purrs when you look at it.'

Givenchy's close relationship with his clients crossed the line between discreet couturier and close friend: Jacqueline Kennedy, who he dressed in ivory satin for a party in Versailles in 1961; the Duchess of Windsor, for whom he made a black dress and coat for her husband's funeral in 1972 in 48 hours; Audrey Hepburn, who Givenchy dressed for almost 40 years after they met at the time he was presenting his first collection. When Givenchy celebrated 40 years in fashion in October 1991 with an exhibition at the Palais Galliéra (Musée de la Mode et du Costume, Paris), naturally it was Hepburn, who had been transformed from gamine film star to ambassador for the United Nations Children's Fund (UNICEF), who inaugurated it.

Givenchy sold his house to LVMH (Louis Vuitton Moët Hennessy) in 1988, after 36 years of being his own boss. With his retirement imminent, the man who Marc Bohan called 'the aristocrat of the couture', told the *Independent*, 'I hope someone exciting and new will replace me. It's important that an established hand is not imprinted on the house – we have to look forward.' John Galliano was appointed Givenchy's successor in 1995, followed by Alexander McQueen in 1996.

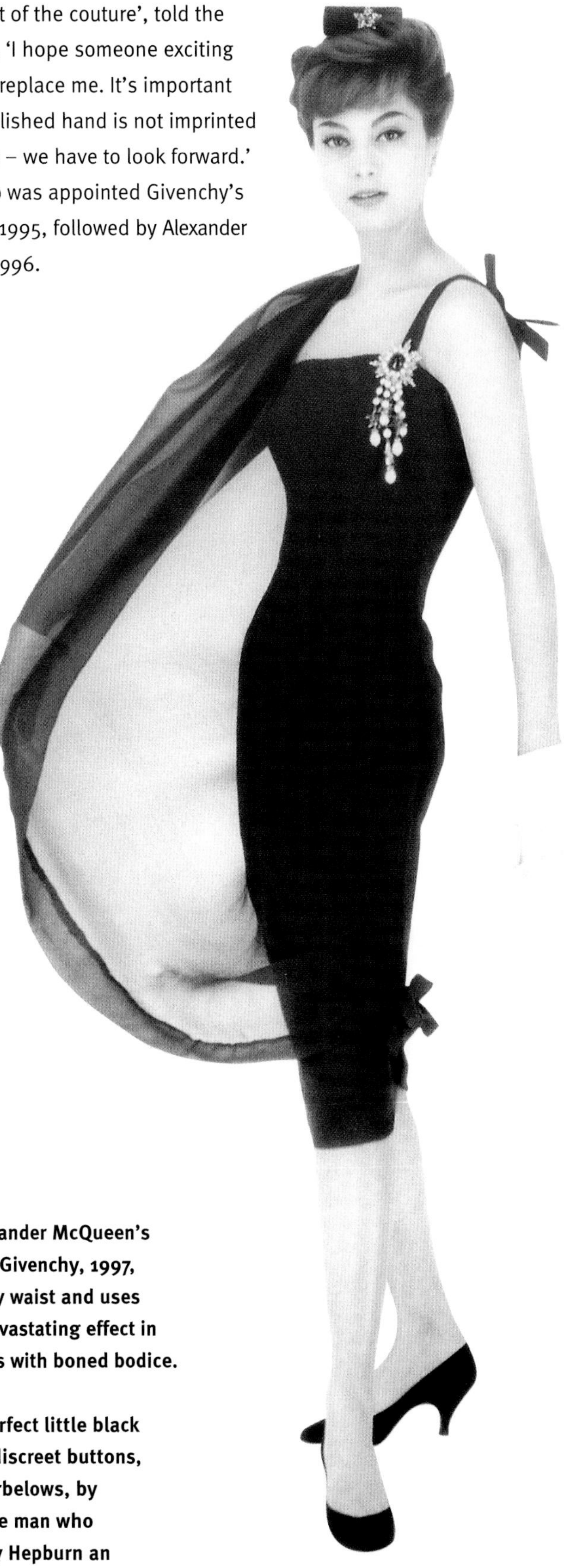

OPPOSITE Alexander McQueen's direction for Givenchy, 1997, creates a tiny waist and uses leather to devastating effect in his minidress with boned bodice.

ABOVE The perfect little black dress, with discreet buttons, bows and furbelows, by Givenchy, the man who made Audrey Hepburn an icon of elegance.

GODLEY, Georgina

BORN: LONDON, ENGLAND, 1955

Georgina Godley's design career was short and sharp, her clothes sculptural and memorable. Godley originally trained as a fine artist at Brighton Polytechnic, moving on to Chelsea School of Art, London. She worked as a restorer and illustrator, and made clothes and sculptures via private commissions before joining forces with fellow student, Scott Crolla, in 1981. They opened Crolla – a menswear shop which specialized in opulent suits. By 1987 Godley was doing her own thing: 'I do believe in a reappraisal of sexual roles,' she told *Vogue* in 1987. 'But we're different and please let's accept it.' Godley is now teaching womenswear at the Royal College of Art in London.

GREER, Howard

BORN: NEBRASKA, USA, 1896
DIED: CALIFORNIA, USA, 1974

Author of *Designing Male*, published in 1951, which told of the trials and tribulations of dressing some of Hollywood's most enduring stars, Howard Greer began his career in the New York branch of Lucile. During the First World War he was stationed in France and gained employment with Paul Poiret and Edward Molyneux. On his return to America, in 1923, he began designing for Paramount and opened his own salon in 1927, using his expertise to re-create his cinematic touches in a realistic setting.

GRÈS, Madame

BORN: PARIS, FRANCE, 1903
DIED: SOUTH OF FRANCE, FRANCE, 1993

'Grès: the supreme dressmaker at the top of her form. Completely modern – sexy, romantic without a trace of nostalgia ... a feeling for splendour and mystery. Her cuts are dreams of invention ... cloth made to move like the extension of a gesture,' observed American *Vogue* in 1964 of the couturier's couturière. Madame Grès trained as a sculptor, studying painting and sculpture in Paris, and served a three-month apprenticeship with the designer Premet in 1930. She worked under the name 'Alix' until 1942 when she adopted her husband's name – he was called Serge Czerefkov, but signed himself Grès. Madame Grès opened her couture house in 1934, which initially consisted of three rooms on rue de Miromesnil, but she soon moved to a three-storey building on avenue Matignon. It was called the

house Alix, on the suggestion of her financial backers. When war broke out in 1940 Madame Grès left Paris. She told *Vogue* in 1984, 'During the war I was in the mountains, the Pyrenees, and I made my own dummies with hay, a bit of wood and a tin. I bought fabric from the market and carried on draping clothes.' After the war she re-established herself as Madame Grès instead of her tradename, Alix, and continued to design along the same lines, taking inspiration from Grecian drapes.

In 1966 *Vogue* recorded a memorable meeting between Madame Grès and Barbra Streisand for a photoshoot with Richard Avedon. 'Grès arrives and a remarkable romantic confrontation it turns out to be: a meeting of two arts, generations, and continents; one epitomizes France, the other all we think of as American. Madame Grès, elegant, luminous, composed, Streisand, fluid, flamboyant and posed; one in classic sweater, skirt, turban and pearls, the other in a huge flowing poncho, a white nunnish coif, looking as though she had been designed by Le Corbusier.'

Notoriously secretive, her death was concealed from the public until the following year, when an exhibition dedicated to her design was held at the Metropolitan Museum of Art, New York. Cecil Beaton once commented: 'She made a Greek dress in a way no Greek could ever have imagined and turned her customers into moving sculptures.'

ABOVE **Madame Grès's slip dress in shirred chiffon and silver-braided, flared metallic coat which 'shoots you straight into the news'.**

OPPOSITE **Pale rose mousseline 'just caught the shoulders', by Madame Grès, the doyenne of draping, cutting and simplicity, 1975.**

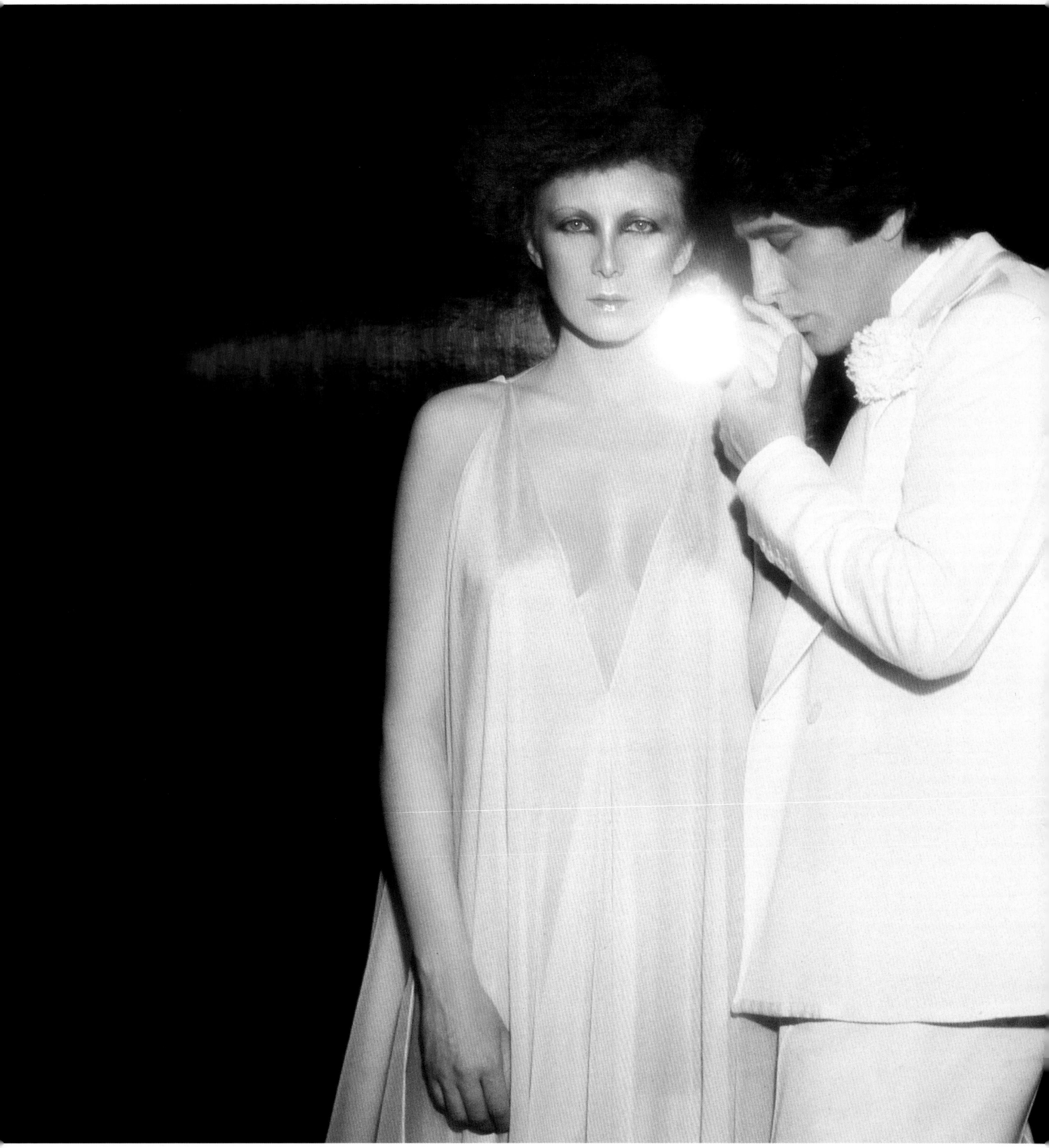

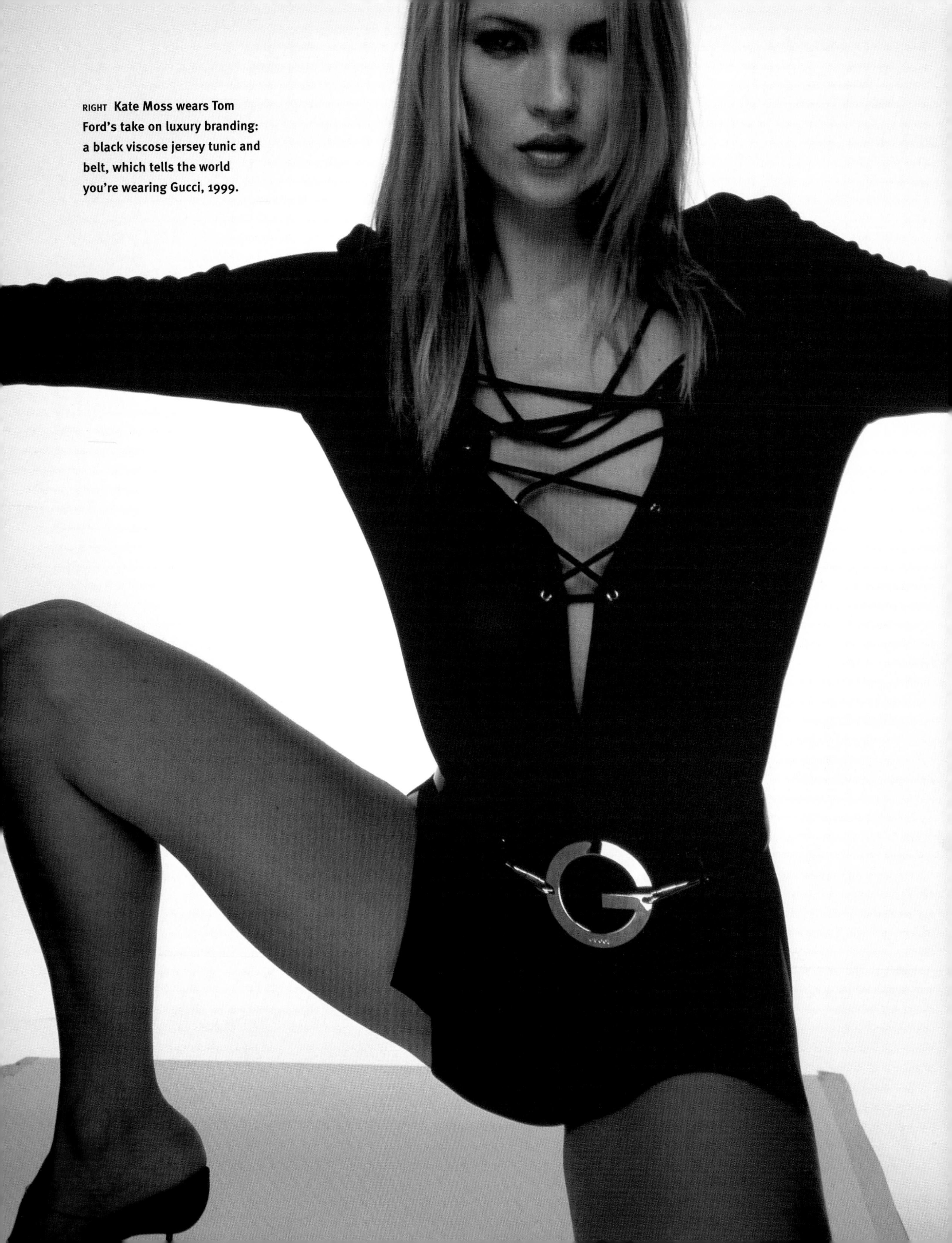

RIGHT **Kate Moss wears Tom Ford's take on luxury branding: a black viscose jersey tunic and belt, which tells the world you're wearing Gucci, 1999.**

GRIFFE, Jacques

BORN: CARCASSONNE, FRANCE, 1917

One of the few designers to have worked at the house of Vionnet, the undisputed queen of perfect cutting, Jacques Griffe, first learnt how to sew and construct clothes under the instruction of his mother. He later trained with a tailor and worked in a couture house before joining Vionnet in 1936. After the Second World War he assisted Edward Molyneux and eventually opened his own house with the encouragement of Vionnet. Despite his earlier training in the art of couture, Griffe could adapt to the mass market and he opened a boutique and also designed a ready-to-wear range, both of which were commercial successes. Nan Kempner, American socialite and front-row fixture, wore a Jacques Griffe dress for her coming out. Later on, she incorporated it into her wedding dress.

GUCCI, Guccio

BORN: FLORENCE, ITALY, 1881
DIED: MILAN, ITALY, 1953

Gucci was originally a leather goods company founded by Guccio Gucci in Florence in 1922. Gucci, who worked as the maître d' at the Savoy in London from 1915 before returning to Florence, knew the importance of service and good quality. He invented the signature interlocking Gs and the red and green trim. In recent years the Gucci label has enjoyed a renaissance of gargantuan proportions. The design director, Tom Ford, appointed in 1994, has pulled off what every financier dreams of: reinvigorating an established house while retaining its identity.

In 1989, following the trend for established houses to be injected with new life, Dawn Mello, who had been president of Bergdorf Goodman for 15 years, took up an offer to move to Italy to become creative director of the label that had gone to sleep and was in desperate need of re-merchandizing. Mello kick-started the Gucci rebirth in 1992. Bestsellers included reinterpretations of the classics of the 1960s: loafers, bamboo bag and leather wallet with hand-shaped silver clasp. Mello rejoined Bergdorf Goodman in 1994 and her ready-to-wear designer, a Texan called Tom Ford, took Gucci from sleepy status-symbol to celebrity must-have. He has a hands-on approach with everything from handbags to his shops' interiors.

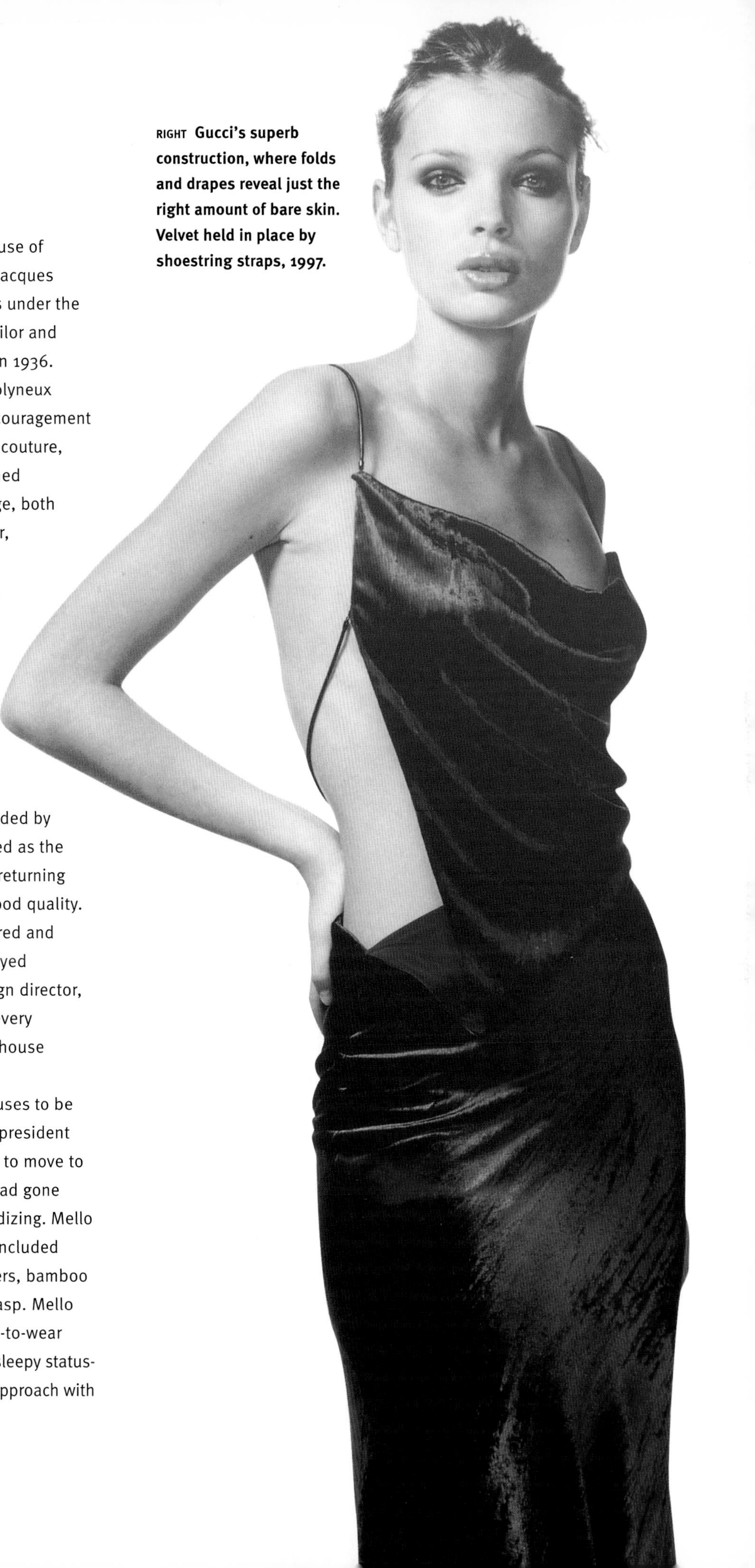

RIGHT Gucci's superb construction, where folds and drapes reveal just the right amount of bare skin. Velvet held in place by shoestring straps, 1997.

HALSTON, Roy Frowick

BORN: DES MOINES, IOWA, USA, 1932
DIED: SAN FRANCISCO, CALIFORNIA, USA, 1990

Roy Halston was New York's most visible party animal during the 1970s and one of the key players in Andy Warhol's infamous diaries. He was a born socialite, fabulous designer and a public relations' dream, who knew the power of the celebrity endorsement. His favourite phrase: 'You're only as good as the people you dress.'

Roy Halston Frowick (as he was christened) arrived in New York in 1958 to assist the milliner Lilly Daché, having already worked in Chicago as a milliner. In the early 1960s, he left Daché to work for Bergdorf Goodman. 'I liked hats,' Halston told *Vogue* in 1972. 'Bergdorf had the biggest millinery business in the world. We had the Who's Who of the world coming to us, from Balenciaga to Givenchy.' Halston was attributed with making Jacqueline Kennedy's first pillbox hat.

On 2 December 1968 Halston opened his salon. Custom quickly followed: avid admirers included Babe Paley, Ali MacGraw and Liza Minelli. By 1973 he had won four Coty Awards and business was booming, reaching almost $30 million retail. He was so famous that he had his own one-off show, *Dinner with Halston*, and in January 1978 he moved his operation to the Olympic Tower, a minimalist palace with panoramic views across Manhattan. In 1983 Halston made the fatal mistake of selling his name. By

BERRY BERENSON

HALSTON

LEFT Halston, 'star designer USA', four times winner of the Coty Award, drawn by Antonio, 1973. Above, Berry Berenson wears his 'easy, rich' suit.

RIGHT The 'New American Look' from Halston in 1973: hand-painted batik stripes on chiffon pyjamas modelled by Berry Berenson, sister of Marissa.

autumn 1984 his Olympic Tower showroom was being sold, and he was working from home. 'Where did Halston go so wrong when he sold his name?' wrote Warhol in his diary entry for 25 November 1984. 'What should he have done that he didn't? That's what I want to know. And I want to know it from him.'

HAMNETT, Katharine

BORN: GRAVESEND, ENGLAND, 1948

'The only way you can change the system is from within,' said Katharine Hamnett in *Vogue* in 1987. 'The next era of conquest is to go into the boardroom wearing a smarter suit than the chairman.' Hamnett is a diplomat's daughter, who was educated at the genteel Cheltenham Ladies College and spent the swinging sixties at the centre of fashion activity, Central Saint Martins College of Art and Design. She was co-founder of Tuttabanken Sportswear in 1970, and when the business folded she designed freelance in New York, Paris, Rome and London, finally founding Katharine Hamnett Limited in 1979 with a £500 loan. She survived bankruptcy and fashion fracas to branch into menswear in 1982.

Her style was always sportswear – jumpsuits made from parachute silk, for example – but it was fashion with a political slant which made her name. In 1983 Hamnett launched her 'Choose Life' T-shirt collection, which was a milestone in the cross-fertilization of fashion and politics. Already a staunch supporter of the Greenham Common women and environmental issues, Hamnett was photographed meeting the prime minister, Margaret Thatcher, at a Downing Street reception in her '58% don't want Pershing' T-shirt. This was a seminal moment in British fashion and the ultimate photo opportunity, resulting in the image of the decade. Other slogans included 'Stop Killing Whales', 'Education Not Missiles', 'Stop Acid Rain', 'Preserve the Rain Forest' and 'Worldwide Nuclear Ban Now', which were all printed in huge capital letters on white T-shirts – a clever ploy to encourage copyists – the British profits from which went towards stopping child abuse. The following year, she received the British Designer of the Year Award and in 1988 the British Knitting and Clothing Export Council Award for Export. In October 1990 she made her Paris debut and launched Hamnett Active and the environmental Green Cotton campaign at the same time.

Katharine Hamnett is a designer with conviction and a company that has an annual turnover of £100 million and

17 licences. In 1992 she wore a 'Vote Tactically' T-shirt and told the *Independent*, 'It's time we got the broom out and swept the cupboard clean: the Tories have actually wrecked the country from top to bottom.' By 1998, disillusioned with New Labour, she defected to the Conservatives and produced a T-shirt that read 'Say No to Euro'.

BELOW 'No message, but brilliant silks', courtesy of Katharine Hamnett – flying colours, tight-waisted dress, scarlet anorak and wind-blown green scarf.

HARTNELL, Sir Norman

BORN: HONITON, ENGLAND, 1901
DIED: WINDSOR, ENGLAND, 1979

In 1939 *Vogue* made the following assessment of royal couturier Norman Hartnell: 'He discovered the lost arts of femininity, and in the arid angularity of the 'twenties, he launched a new, de luxe woman, poised, svelte and soignée: subtle rather than snappy.'

Romanticism was Hartnell's signature, and was perfectly suited to Cecil Beaton's Winterhalter-inspired images of the Windsors surrounded by garlands of flowers and an air of mystique. Hartnell's distinguished career started at Magdalene College, Cambridge, where his costumes and posters for the amateur dramatic societies received favourable reviews and caught the imagination of Lady Diana Duff-Cooper, who persuaded him to exchange academia for the more insecure world of haute couture. He took a job for £3 per week with the court dressmaker Madame Desirée and was sacked three months later. Undeterred, in 1923 he opened his own dressmaking studio at 10 Bruton Street, London, with his sister, three workgirls, a sewing machine and £300 capital from his father. He took his collection to Paris in 1927.

Appointed dressmaker to Queen Elizabeth in 1937, Hartnell excelled at grand occasions – he designed the gown worn by the Queen Mother for the portrait by Cecil Beaton (opposite) and two royal wedding dresses. The first, for Princess Elizabeth in 1947, was embroidered with 10,000 seed pearls and diamonds and was described by *Vogue* as 'ivory satin, starred with Botticelli-like delicacy and richness with pearl and crystal roses, wheat, orange blossom'. The second, for Princess Margaret's wedding to the then photographer Tony Armstrong Jones in 1960, was probably the most beautiful royal wedding dress ever made, a masterpiece in white silk organza, which silenced the critics who said Hartnell's forte was glitz. He designed the Queen's historic white satin coronation dress of 1952, which was embroidered with emblems of Great Britain and the Commonwealth, including a Welsh leek and a Canadian maple leaf. 'It is not sensible to be too sensible in fashion, nor is it smart to be too smart,' he commented in 1964. Royals apart, Hartnell's clientele included Merle Oberon, Marlene Dietrich, Evelyn Laye and Gertrude Lawrence. In 1977 Hartnell was awarded Knight Commander of the Royal Victorian Order – the first time a couturier had been honoured with the Queen's personal gift of knighthood. He was responsible for the wardrobe of Queen Elizabeth the Queen Mother for over half a century.

In 1987, eight years after the death of its founder, the house was acquired by former Moss Bros chief executive, Manny Silverman, who initially brought in British designer Murray Arbeid and, later, Victor Edelstein. In June 1990 Silverman persuaded Marc Bohan, ex-head of Dior for 28 years, to move to Hartnell. His first Hartnell collection was unveiled in January 1991 to great acclaim. Unfortunately, even the seasoned skills and considerable talent of Bohan could not save Hartnell and its salon in Bruton Street, closed in November 1992.

HEAD, Edith

BORN: LOS ANGELES, CALIFORNIA, USA, 1907
DIED: LOS ANGELES, CALIFORNIA, USA, 1981

Meticulous, bilingual and mesmeric, Edith Head was a prolific and revered designer, who became the first female to run a costume department in the history of Hollywood.

An only child who spent her early years in Mexico, Head eventually moved back to Los Angeles to study at the University of California, and then took an MA at Stanford University, where she specialized in languages. She taught Spanish at the Hollywood School for Girls and began studying life drawing and sculpture in the evenings.

Her illustrious career started in 1923 at Paramount Studios when she became assistant to Howard Greer and then to his successor Travis Banton. In 1938 Banton left to become freelance and Head was appointed the first female head of a studio. In 1967 she became chief designer at Universal Studios. Head studied cinema from all angles, analysing the script, the stars and the action, and meticulously researching the period in which the films were set. She frequently worked on several films – both historical and contemporary – simultaneously.

Highlights of her career included dressing Clara Bow, Mae West, Veronica Lake and Shirley Temple. She designed the famous sarong for Dorothy Lamour in *The Jungle Princess* (1936) and dressed Charles Laughton as Nero in *The Sign of the Cross* (1932). Edith Head collected eight Oscars, including one for her costumes for Gloria Swanson in *Sunset Boulevard* and another for *All About Eve*, both in 1950. Speaking after the Second World War she said, 'I honestly don't mind when people say to me, "Remember the fantastic clothes you used to design?" After all, it was the fabulous era, and the movies were very young.'

OPPOSITE **The Queen Mother – 100 years old in the year 2000 – poses for Cecil Beaton 'in unaccustomed black' velvet dress by Norman Hartnell, 1949.**

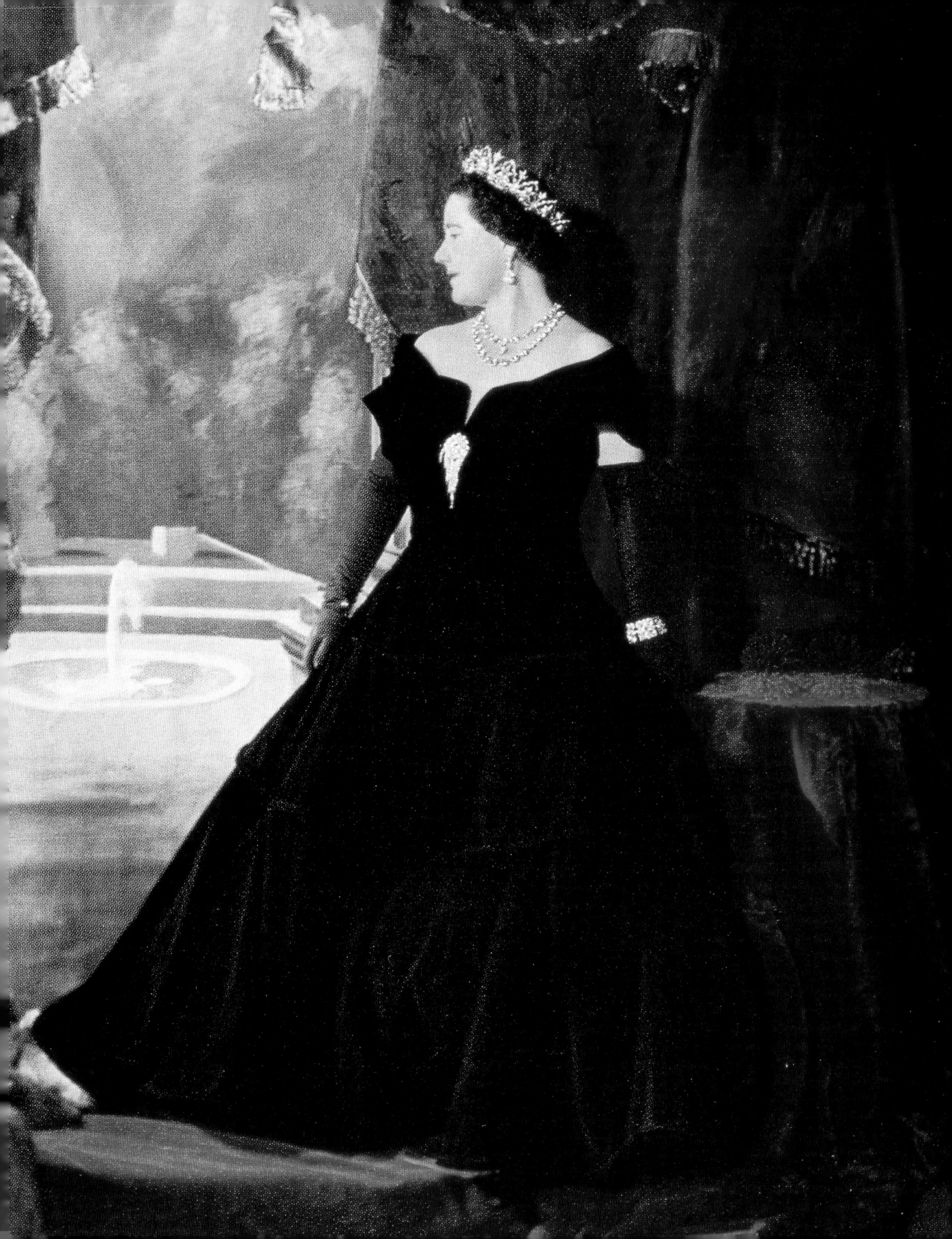

HEIM, Jacques

BORN: PARIS, FRANCE, 1899
DIED: PARIS, FRANCE, 1967

In the 1920s Jacques Heim managed his parents' fur fashion house and started a couture branch before opening his own couture house in 1930. Heim is considered more of a marketer than a designer, who was able to adapt and survive in a fickle business for almost 40 years. He launched a diffusion line in 1950 and was elected president of the Chambre Syndicale de la Couture Parisienne in 1958. Heim held the position until 1962, when he upset his fellow designers by disclosing their collections to the American press before the agreed date. His business closed two years after his death in 1969.

HERMÈS

FOUNDED BY THIERRY HERMÈS IN 1837

Thierry Hermès established himself as a master craftsman with a workshop in rue Basse du Rampart, Paris, making harnesses to sell to the carriage-makers of the Champs Elysées. Saddlery was added in 1879 and the business moved to 24 Faubourg-Saint-Honoré, where the flagship shop still stands. Thierry's grandsons, Adolphe and Emile-Maurice, spread the Hermès name wordwide, supplying the Imperial Court of Russia and clients in South America. After the First World War and the demise of the horse-drawn carriage, Hermès made small leather goods – wallets, handbags and luggage. In 1922 Emile-Maurice bought his brother's share of the business and the building. Leather goods were soon followed by clothing, costume jewellery, diaries and silk squares printed with original designs, the first of which appeared in 1937. In the late 1950s a fragrance division was launched.

In 1988 Claude Brouet was appointed design director and was responsible for the renaissance of the revamped Kelly bag – named after Princess Grace of Monaco – a cult handbag of the 1950s. Martin Margiela was appointed to design the ready-to-wear collection in 1997.

HILFIGER, Tommy

BORN: ELMIRA, NEW YORK, USA, 1952

The Tommy Hilfiger Corporation was founded in New York in 1992 and it is a label that appeals to young and old. In the best traditions of American design, where business, design and marketing are mutually compatible, Hilfiger is an unashamed marketing magnate, who knows his customers and what they want – relaxed, comfortable sportswear. He expanded his line in 1994 with tailoring.

HOWELL, Margaret

BORN: REIGATE, ENGLAND, 1946

'Quality is like coffee. Once you've tried the real thing, you can't go back to instant,' said Margaret Howell. Quality is the cornerstone of her business and her collections always centre on the eternals: white shirt, trenchcoat and classic trousers. She is one of the few female designers with flair for designing both mens- and womenswear, and she also designs household, gardening and children's merchandise.

Howell studied fine art at Goldsmith's College, University of London, and began designing accessories. She developed her first clothing collection in 1970 and opened her flagship shop during the 1980s. Howell was nominated Designer of the Year by *Vogue*'s editor Grace Coddington. Her clothes are displayed in the Costume Museum in Bath and in the Victoria and Albert Museum in London.

LEFT **Hermès, plain and simple under the precise direction of Martin Margiela, is taking luxury into the millennium.**

LEFT **A silk chiffon dress, sleeveless white linen shirt – totally devoid of fuss or frippery and typically Margaret Howell, 1986.**

BELOW **Naomi Campbell in a simple shirt with cropped, iridescent trousers by Marc Jacobs, who designs for Louis Vuitton, 1999.**

JACOBS, Marc

BORN: NEW YORK, NEW YORK, USA, 1964

One of America's most celebrated young guns, Marc Jacobs has risen – in the space of 15 years – from Parson's graduate to design director of the revered luxury goods line, Louis Vuitton. Jacobs graduated from Parson's School of Design in New York and won the Perry Ellis Golden Thimble Award in 1984. He started his own company – which lasted for two years – before taking up a post at Perry Ellis, following in the footsteps of one of America's foremost sportswear designers. In 1994, Jacobs formulated his own line, which still continues to receive rave reviews for its simplicity and modernity. He was announced designer at Louis Vuitton in 1997 and told American *Vogue* of his plans: 'What I have in mind are things that are deluxe but that you can also throw into a bag and escape town with, because Louis Vuitton has its heritage in travel.'

JACKSON, Betty

BORN: BACUP, ENGLAND, 1949

After graduating from the Royal College of Art, London, Betty Jackson began her career via the Quorum design studio. She set up her own business in 1981 with her husband, David Cohan, who is also a director of the company. Jackson was awarded an MBE in 1987 and opened her first retail outlet after a decade in business in September 1991 in London's Brompton Cross. She has never had a backer.

Jackson's style is fluid and easy; she achieves a thoughtful balance between fashion and comfort, and her uncomplicated shapes often incorporate printed textiles and tactile fabrics such as suede, muslin jersey, silk georgette and hand-beaded silk. Her oversized shirts, which hide a multitude of sins, are always the first pieces to sell out. Jackson's clothes are sold in Europe, the USA and the Middle and Far East. She also produces BJ accessories and BJ knits, and has been a consultant on womenswear for high street chain, Marks and Spencer. Customers range from British comediennes to serious thespians. She admires strong women, 'like Lauren Bacall', she told *Vogue* in 1991, 'Bold and casual. I've never liked prettiness much.'

LEFT 'Sharp, white fluorescent jacket, with silver buttons all the way,' 1966. From Betsey Johnson, former 1960s' swinger, now flower child.

OPPOSITE 'The Hots', 1988: Stephen Jones's parti-coloured check, fine straw pork pie hat, perched precariously on the side of the head.

JONES, Stephen

BORN: WEST KIRBY, ENGLAND, 1957

Having graduated from London's Central Saint Martins College of Art and Design at a pivotal time in British fashion – post-punk and pre-New Romantics – milliner Stephen Jones designed a collection for Fiorucci before opening his first salon in Covent Garden, London, in September 1980.

Educated at Liverpool College in 1975, he completed his art foundation course at High Wycombe School of Art. His collections have included miniature Christmas trees and swirling meringues, and reflected mood swings from 'Norma Desmond Lives' (1992) to 'Murder by Millinery' (1997).

Jones has designed for many international names including Jean Paul Gaultier, John Galliano, Thierry Mugler, Zandra Rhodes, Claude Montana and Vivienne Westwood. His hats have been worn by a host of celebrities – from Madonna to U2. He designed hats for Disney's *101 Dalmations* (1996) and Steven Spielberg's *Jurassic Park* (1993).

Temporarily eclipsed by the arrival of Philip Treacy at the turn of the 1990s, Jones continues to create innovative and outlandish hats and also has licences for gloves, scarves and eyewear, in addition to Jonesgirl for Stephen Jones Japan. He has produced a collection of asymmetric shapes specifically to celebrate the Millennium on New Year's Eve, and is credited with helping to revive the art of millinery during the latter part of the twentieth century.

JOHNSON, Betsey

BORN: WETHERSFIELD, CONNECTICUT, USA, 1942

At the same time that Mary Quant was causing a stir in London, Betsey Johnson was creating a Carnaby Street situation in New York, gaining a reputation as a radical young designer, selling a clear vinyl dress with paste-your-own star motifs.

She studied at the Pratt Institute, New York, and originally intended to become a dancer. Her first boutique was called Betsey, Bunky and Nini. An advocate of flower power, she married John Cale of the Velvet Underground.

Betsey Johnson has been a colourful fixture on the New York scene for 20 years, often doing a cartwheel down the catwalk – not bad for a woman pushing 60. She showed her first London collection in 1998. Her daughter, Lulu, a more restrained blonde, designs the Betsey Johnson Ultra collection.

JOURDAN, Charles

FOUNDED BY CHARLES JOURDAN IN 1920

The Charles Jourdan label – founded in Romans, France, in 1920 – has always been able to swing according to the way fashion is going. In the 1950s Jourdan created the high beechwood heel, the 1960s produced the patent leather pump with circular heel, rounded toe and daisy on the front, and in the 1970s the ubiquitous platforms appeared. These were shown to their best advantage in advertising campaigns shot by photographer Guy Bourdin.

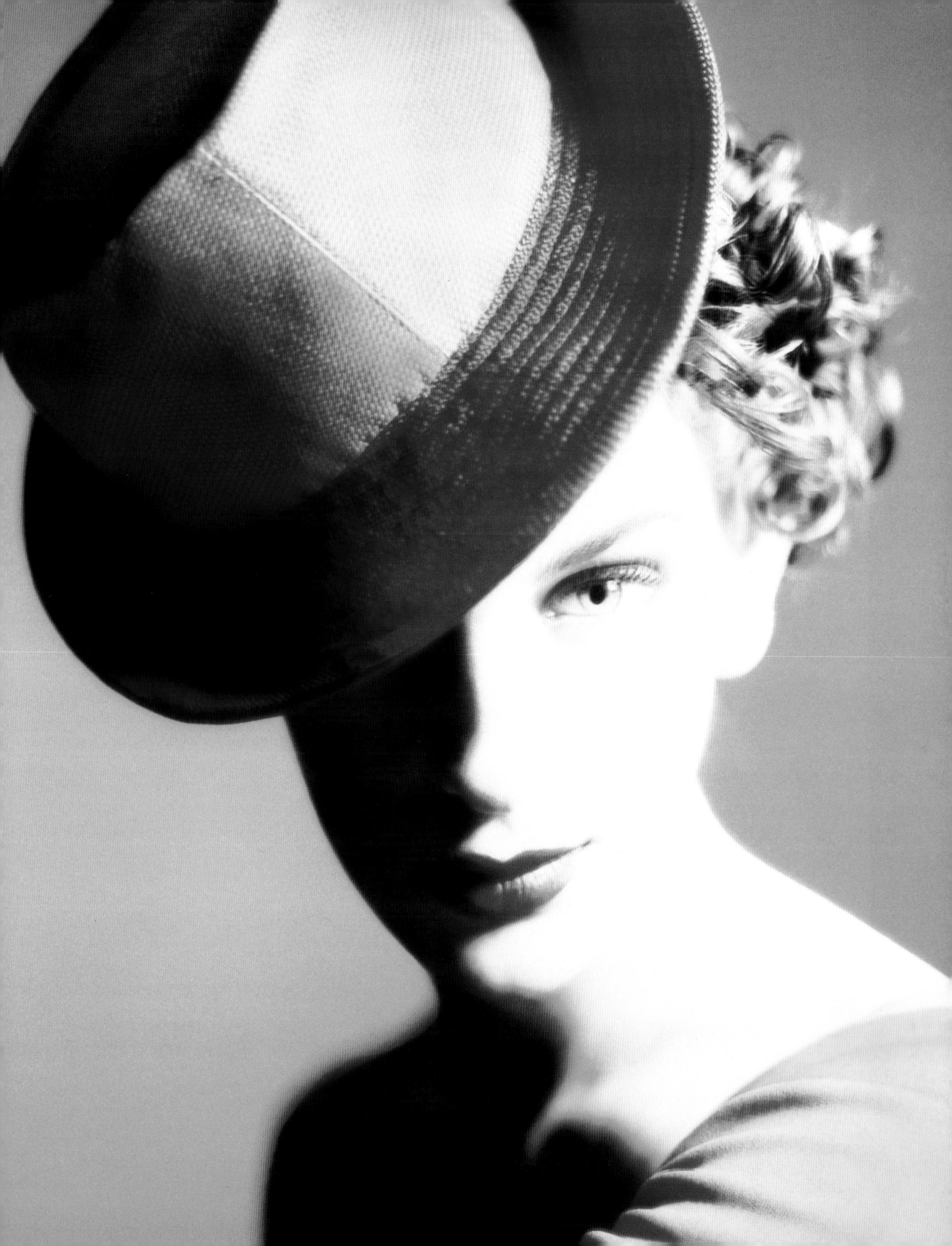

KAMALI, Norma

BORN: NEW YORK, NEW YORK, USA, 1945

A native New Yorker, whose flagship store stands in Madison Avenue, Norma Kamali successfully mixes modernism with nostalgia. She has won two CFDA Awards for video innovation and designed costumes for the Twyla Tharp Company and for the Emerald City sequence in Sidney Lumet's *The Wiz* (1978). Kamali left New York's Fashion Institute of Technology in 1964 with a degree in fashion illustration. Four years later she opened her own shop at 229 East 53rd Street. Her first designs were typical of the late 1960s, combining appliquéd leather, lizard and snakeskin. She pared down her designs as the 1970s progressed, making clothes from silk parachutes as early as 1974, and her famous sleeping-bag coat the following year. Her shop OMO (On My Own) opened in 1978 after her divorce.

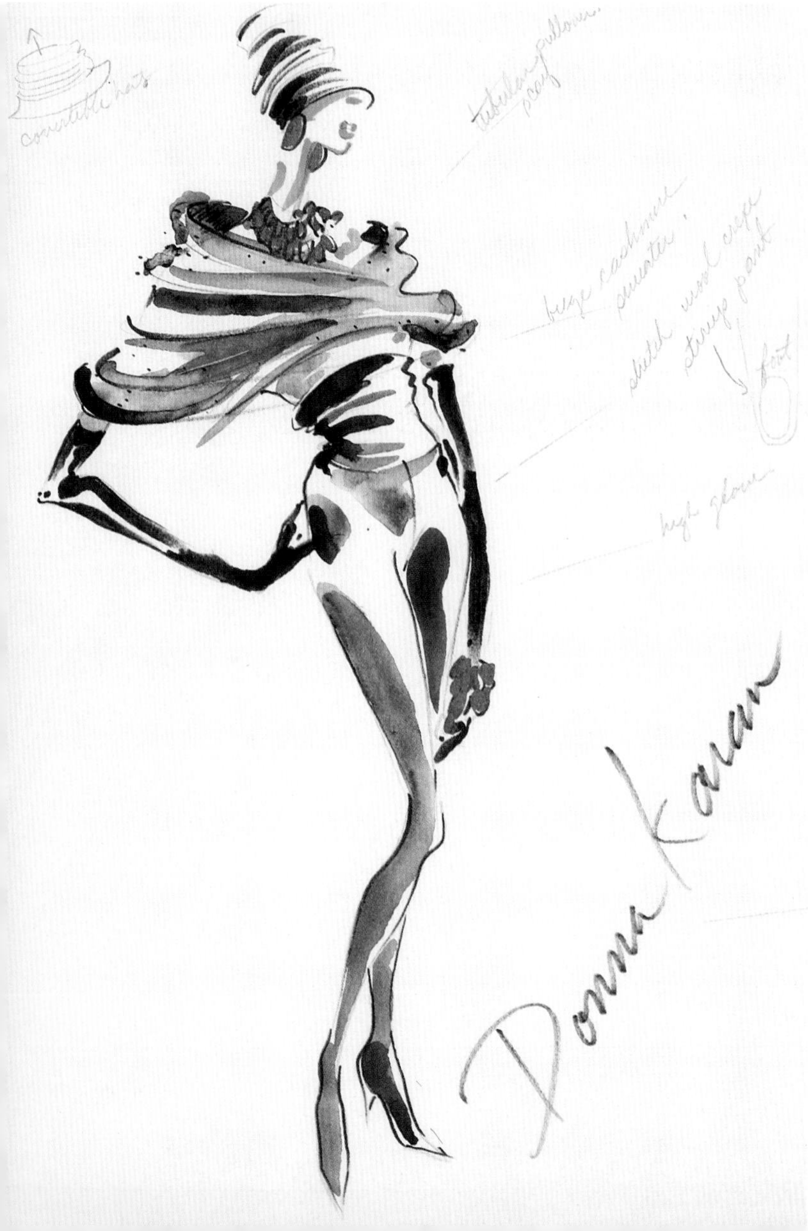
Donna Karan

KARAN, Donna

BORN: LONG ISLAND, NEW YORK, USA, 1948

Donna Karan built her business on three things: a stretch body, a sarong skirt and precise pieces of bold jewellery. She added neutral colours, a measure of stretch and assembled a philosophy which was alien to social X-Rays. As she told *Vogue* in July 1987, 'I am a woman with a rounded figure. I'm not a model size 8. I won't design clothes that can't be worn by a woman who is a size 12 or 14.'

Karan started her career as assistant to Anne Klein in 1967, but it was almost 20 years later, in 1985, when she formed her own company. When Karan acknowledged the existence of hips and curves and said, 'I'm dealing with the fallibility of a woman's body', she struck a chord with half the population on the planet.

Like all successful American designers, Donna Karan was backed by powerful advertising campaigns – the most memorable showing a Karan-suited woman being sworn in as president of America. Donna Karan lives the life she sells: Seventh Avenue during the day; East Hampton at weekends; a family and husband; and running an empire. Karan's spring 1993 press release underlined the link between imagination and reality: 'Like her ads, Karan starts the day on the telephone in her car. And from there it's anyone's guess. She could be dashing to a fitting, meeting with her retailers, brainstorming with her ad agency ... or showing her collection to the ladies from *Vogue*.'

Like the analyst who soothes the mind, Karan shoots inspirational one-liners – instant relief to those who aren't ecstatic about their natural outline. Her thoughts on black: 'It goes day-into-evening. It packs. It's city friendly. And you never have to worry about how to dress the leg.' And to the stressed-out executive with ample thighs: 'Once I figure it out for me, I can figure it out for you.' In 1992 she assured readers of American *Vogue*, 'Right now I'm having a catastrophe over legs.'

Karan is not only consumer sensitive, offering an oasis of calm for the bodily challenged, she also knows about the feeling of fabric on skin and loves natural fabrics – her body cream was, appropriately, called Cashmere. Karan doesn't just do stretch, comfort and clever psychology. During her reign on Seventh Avenue she put women into pinstripe suits and brought out a sportier range, DKNY. From the tip of her slingbacks to the sweep of her wrap, Karan keeps to her seasonal mantra: 'Layer. Subtract. Add. Delete.'

LEFT **Donna Karan's formula for the rounded figure, 1987, in jersey, neutral colours and body-conscious stretch, with the ubiquitous, generous wrap.**

OPPOSITE **All that glitters: Donna Karan's weighty gold sequinned sarong, accessorized with pure lilies, Grecian pillars and bare breasts, 1985.**

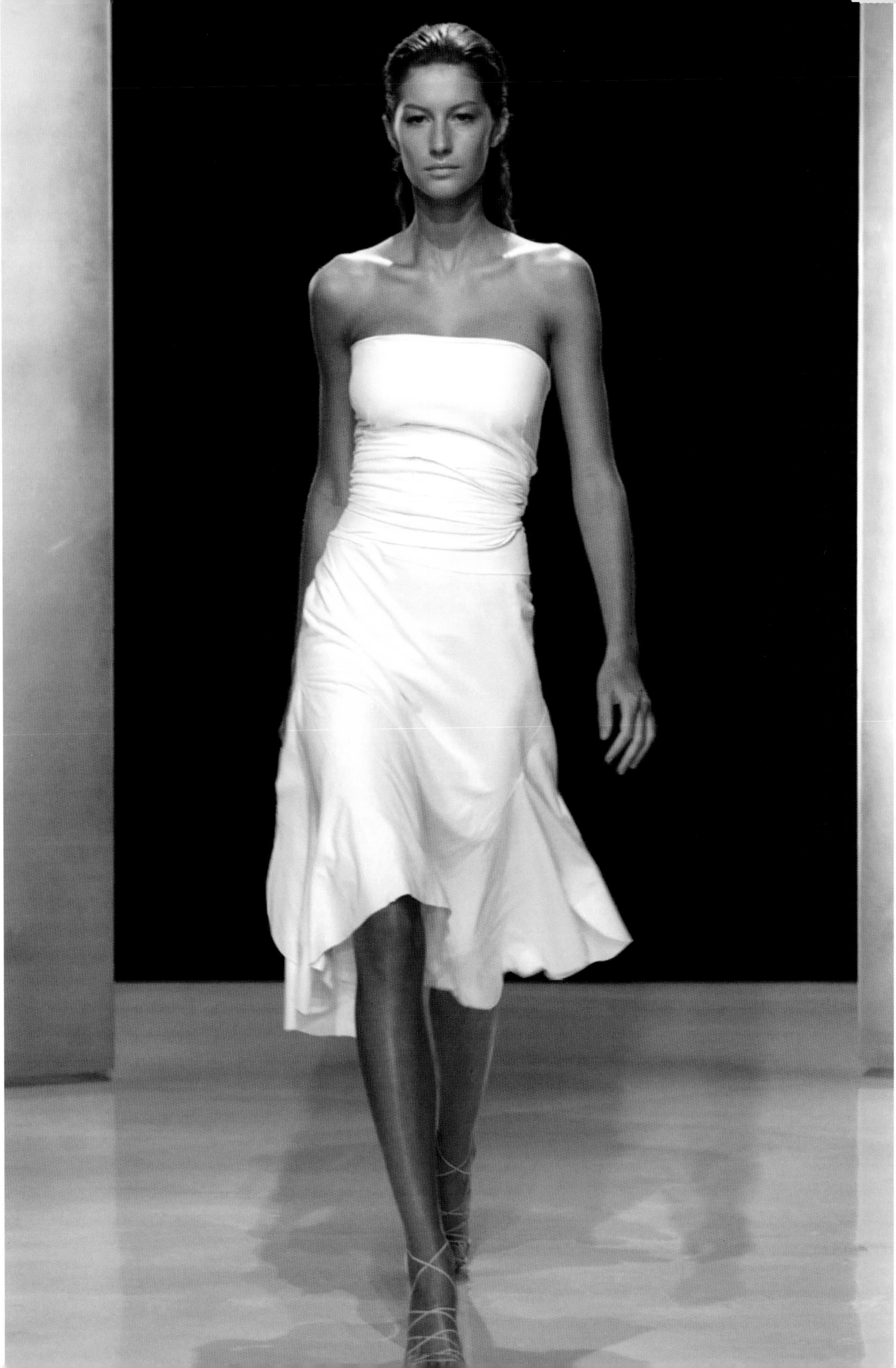

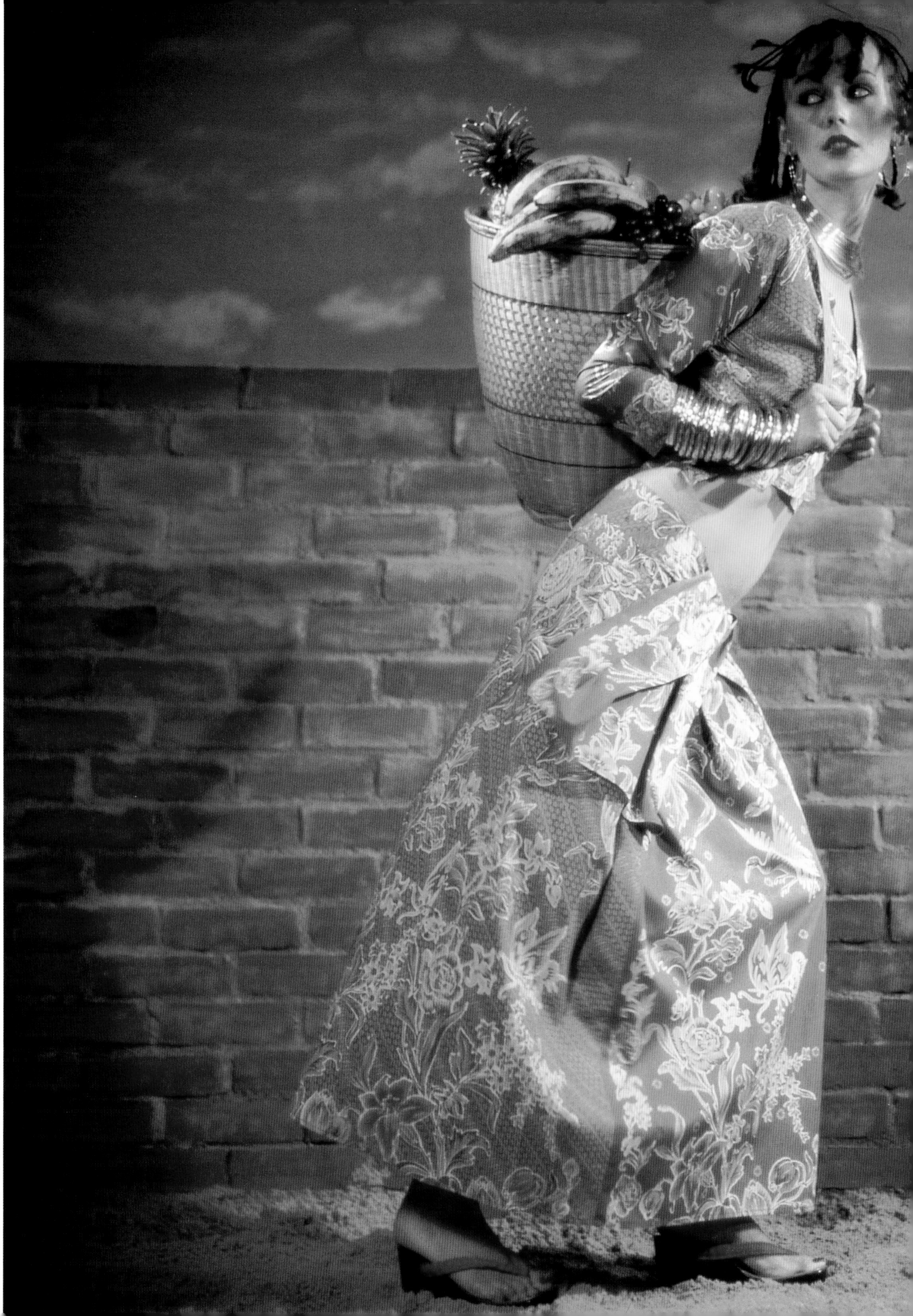

KELLY, Patrick

BORN: VICKSBURG, MISSISSIPPI, USA, 1954
DIED: PARIS, FRANCE, 1990

Huge buttons, abbreviated hemlines and a talent for trompe l'oeil marked Patrick Kelly out as a natural New Yorker in Paris. His colourful clothes were a product of his Mississippi childhood and his long-held fascination with antique clothes. He so impressed his French compatriots that he became the first American designer to be elected to the Chambre Syndicale de la Couture Parisienne.

Kelly studied history at Jackson State University in Mississippi and fashion at Parson's School of Design in New York, but he learnt his trade on the shop floor; this included a stint at a Rive Gauche boutique and a foray into antique clothing. In 1980 Kelly moved to Paris, where he became a freelance costume designer for Le Palais Club. Sadly, Kelly's promising career was cut short by his untimely death.

KENZO

BORN: HYOGO, JAPAN, 1939

A brilliant mix of colour, texture and attention to detail, Kenzo's style regularly crosses the design spectrum: menswear, womenswear, and also costume. He has even been a film director.

Kenzo — full name Kenzo Takada — studied at the Bunka College of Fashion in Tokyo, and worked briefly there before relocating to Paris to work as a freelance designer in 1965. In 1970 he opened his first boutique, Jungle Jap, which immediately attracted customers including models and trendsetters. Money was tight to start off with, and Kenzo's first autumn/winter collection was made entirely of cotton, much of it quilted.

A tireless innovator, Kenzo's lively combination of textures and patterns has spawned a dozen imitators. The Kenzo label was first introduced to London by Joseph Ettedgui, who sold his sweaters in his hairdressing salon, and later in his shops. Unlike his compatriots, Kenzo does not dabble in radical cutting or intellectual dressing, but produces young, wearable collections that are easily understood and worn endlessly.

LEFT **Kenzo's colourful, crisp, and cleverly abbreviated kimono top ties above a bare midriff. Worn with a sarong-style skirt, 1976.**

KEOGH, Lainey

BORN: OLD TOWN, IRELAND, 1957

Creator of the most amazingly organic knitwear, Lainey Keogh spent her childhood living on a farm as part of a family of ten, watching the Irish countryside go by: 'We ate, slept, and lived our lives in tune with the seasons.'

Keogh studied microbiology and was discovered by retailer Marianne Gunn O'Connor while she was knitting in the corner of Bewley's coffee house in Dublin. Her first collection had the buyers in raptures and her first show, in February 1997, was unveiled to great acclaim.

Keogh works mostly with cashmere and, more recently, with crystal. Her pieces are predominantly handmade by expert Irish knitters. 'We do a lot of things through human endeavour,' says the maker of lyrical knits, 'but we are dipping into technology in the millennium.'

KERRIGAN, Daryl

BORN: DUBLIN, IRELAND, 1964

One of the few Irish designers to take New York by storm, Daryl Kerrigan – or Daryl K as she is known to her younger customers – has captured the market in hip, cool sportswear with a SoHo slant.

Kerrigan studied at the National College of Art and Design in Dublin and arrived in New York at the age of 22. She originally worked on costume design in the film industry, most famously dressing Joe Pesci in *My Cousin Vinny* (1992). With her earnings from that project, she opened her own shop in 1992. Kerrigan quickly established herself as a designer who could appeal to the American market, but she was also able to think both laterally and internationally. Her look is East Village elite, with a healthy slice of sportswear. In 1996 she won the CFDA Perry Ellis Award for Womenswear.

KHANH, Emmanuelle

BORN: PARIS, FRANCE, 1937

'The Emmanuelle Khanh cult has spread like wildfire,' wrote *Vogue* in 1964. 'Her gentle, feminine shapes and her curvy tailoring have been copied everywhere.' An ex-model, who showed Givenchy and Balenciaga dresses off to their best advantage during the late 1950s, Emmanuelle Khanh switched to the other side of the fashion business in 1962. She was at the forefront of the French revolution in favour of ready to wear, and is credited with starting the young fashion movement in France.

Khanh's clothes had a hippie feel to them. She first became known for The Droop, a slim, clinging dress which contrasted with the structured clothes of the time. Signature details included Romanian embroidery coupled with denim and chenille, and she also featured dangling cufflink fastenings and half-moon moneybag pockets. Her silhouettes were always refined, flattering and utterly French.

With a great ability to combine colour, detail and commercial acumen, Khanh worked with Cacharel and Dorothée Bis before pursuing a freelance career in the late 1970s.

KLEIN, Anne

BORN: BROOKLYN, NEW YORK, USA, 1923
DIED: NEW YORK, NEW YORK, USA, 1974

Taking her cue from Claire McCardell, Anne Klein epitomized American simplicity. She was one of the first designers to celebrate sportswear as the most workable way to accommodate the typical American woman's lifestyle, using cool fabrics, clean lines and sportswear shapes.

Klein was 15 when she got her first job on Seventh Avenue; the next year she joined Varden Petites and in 1948 she set up her own company with her husband. Given her training, it was natural that she should first fill gaps in the market, and she became known for taking junior-size clothes out of little-girl cuteness and into adult sophistication. In the mid-1960s Klein had already sensed a sea change in women's attitudes towards work, and designed her collections accordingly. She was one of the first designers to have shop floor space dedicated solely to her label – a store within a store – and was the winner of many awards – from Coty American Fashion Critics' Award to an award from the National Cotton Council.

After Klein's death in 1974, the firm continued under Donna Karan, a former design assistant. When Karan left to form her own company in 1985, the label was headed by Louis Dell'Olio, followed by Richard Tyler in 1993.

OPPOSITE **Extraordinary knitwear from Ireland's inventor, Lainey Keogh. Here, her Venus dress is worn with a cashmere coat from Clements Ribeiro, 1998.**

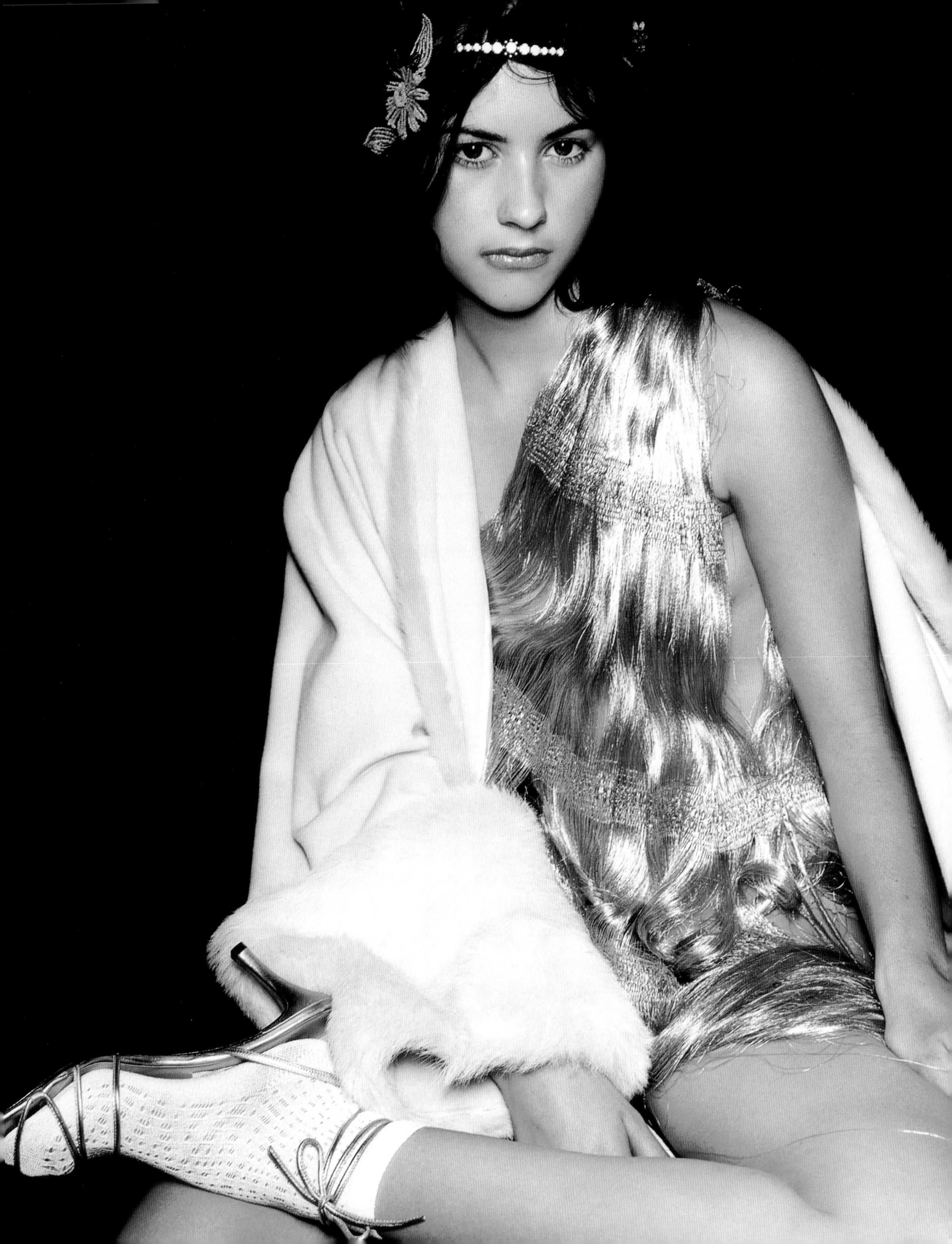

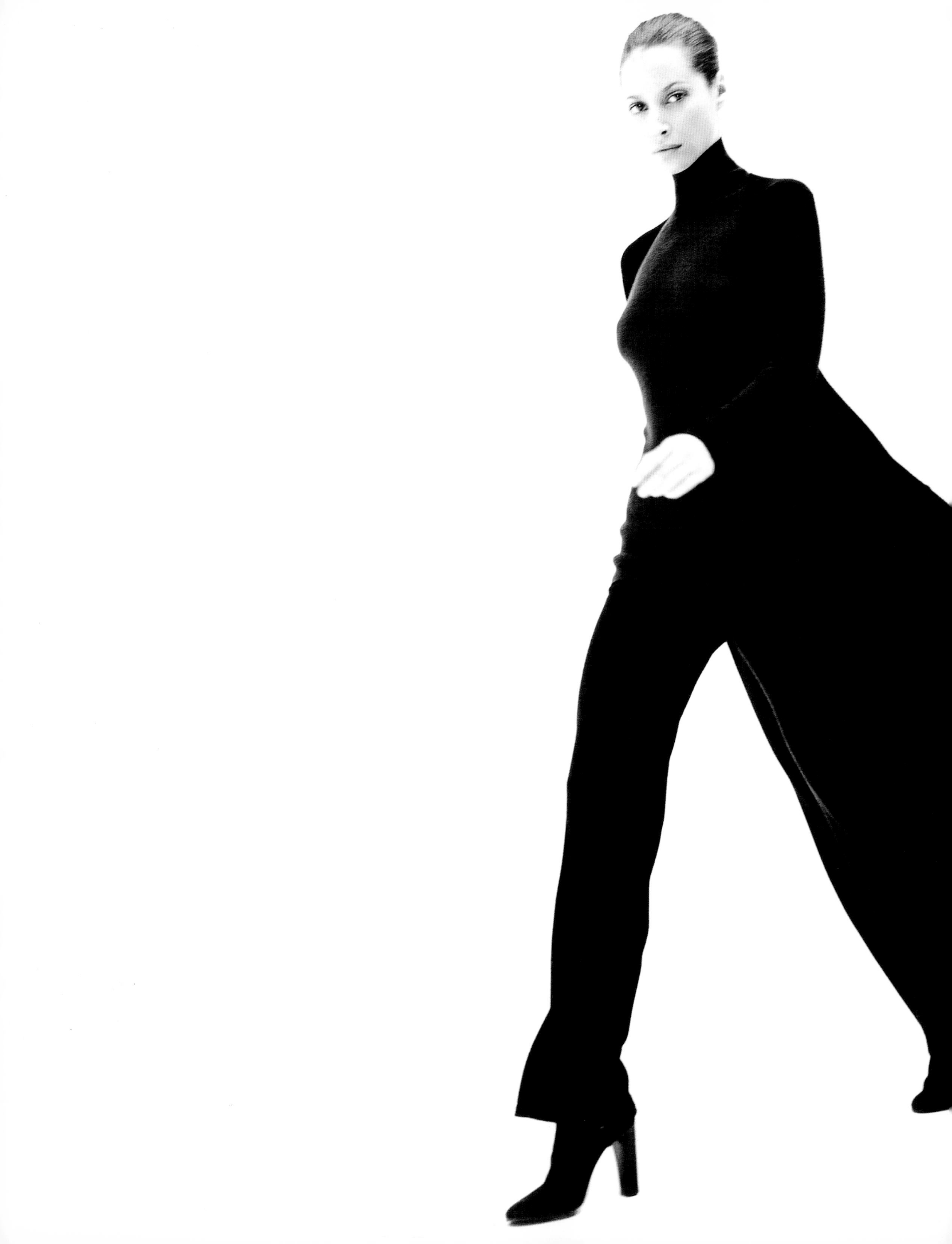

KLEIN, Calvin

BORN: NEW YORK, NEW YORK, USA, 1942

Tapping into the *Zeitgeist* comes naturally to Calvin Klein; some say he directs it. From being at the centre of 1970s disco to the quiet refinement of Long Island's Hamptons, Klein has steered, redesigned and refined the international image of classic American fashion. He frequented the New York nightclub Studio 54 when it was hot; launched designer jeans in the 1970s; reinvented men's underwear in the late 1980s; brought out two fragrances – Obsession and Eternity – one after the other in the 1990s; and was the first designer to pick up on the widespread appeal of supermodel Kate Moss.

Calvin Klein's style has always pivoted on simple, all-American principles of wearable purity: white shirt, classic jeans, camel coat, perfect T-shirt, cable-knit sweater. These are the fashion eternals, which Calvin Klein knows will last into the next century.

Brought up in the Bronx, Klein was educated at the Fashion Institute of Technology in New York, before starting his own business in 1968 with his business partner Barry Schwartz. By the 1970s Klein was enjoying the kind of success his competitors would kill for. His sales zoomed into the outer stratosphere when he employed a teenage Brooke Shields for an advertising campaign; she was shown lying across a billboard wearing blue jeans with the seductive byline, 'Nothing comes between me and my Calvin's'.

No one understood, predicted and rode the designer-obsessed 1980s better than Calvin Klein. Cleverly, no one switched tack more quickly when the 1990s started gliding towards nurturing and nest-building. Klein replaced his minimalist interior for soft cushions and sofas, traded in his batchelor lifestyle for marriage and bought his new wife, Kelly, a gold and diamond eternity ring that once belonged to the Duchess of Windsor.

Like all American designers, Klein's life and design are a single entity. He understood the power of the older woman in the early 1990s, as well as that of the grungy waif. In 1993 he scored a double whammy when he was voted both Mens- and Womenswear Designer of the Year. The common denominator has always been classic Americanism: glossy hair, clear skin,

OPPOSITE 'C is for Christy in Calvin': Klein's clean and totally modern silhouette, 1996 – turtleneck sweater, aubergine cardigan and knitted trousers.

effortless beauty. Naturally, it was Klein who employed the epitome of Calvin Klein's vision, Carolyn Bessette Kennedy, as his PR.

An American marketing genius without compare, Klein understands that the new radicals can do what they want. Shock expires. Reality sells. Everyone wants to be able to sit down, stand up, and put their hands on a perfect American classic every once in a while.

BELOW Palest *café au lait* cashmere polo neck sweater and deep brown suede trousers, tailored like jodhpurs, 1989

LEFT **Michael Kors takes the reins at Céline, producing a luxurious cashmere coat, cashmere sweater and white silk, sequinned skirt for winter 1998.**

KRIZIA

FOUNDED BY MARIUCCIA MANDELLI IN 1954

With Mariuccia Mandelli at the helm, Krizia is one of Italy's most successful and best-known labels. Originally a teacher, Mandelli started making her own clothes, designed a series of separates, and by the mid-1950s was sufficiently established to launch an exhibition of her work. Krizia's design has always mixed the fantastical with the colourful. In the best tradition of Italian fashion, it combines both brilliant texture with wit. Knitwear is a speciality.

LACHASSE, House of

FOUNDED IN 1928

England's oldest couture establishment has survived war, economic fluctuation and every significant trend – from the flapper to deconstruction. Lachasse still has a hard-core client base who remain loyal to the kind of British tailoring in which the house excels – immaculate cutting, fine fabrics, and nothing too radical. An emulator rather than an instigator of fashion, Lachasse remains a resolute favourite with the British aristocracy, who could tell the world a thing or two about good taste.

Lachasse has employed many of the most important British designers during its reign: Digby Morton, Hardy Amies and, during the 1950s, Michael Donellan, who in 1953 was photographed by *Vogue* as part of the Incorporated Society of London Fashion Designers. During the 1980s, Japanese designer Yuki worked upstairs, draping his beautiful evening gowns in a small room above the Lachasse workrooms. Lachasse is still synonymous with the best of British tailoring and is currently under the direction of Peter Lewis-Crown.

KORS, Michael

BORN: NEW YORK, NEW YORK, USA, 1959

Michael Kors is one of the industry's great communicators. He loves doing trunk shows, explaining looks, meeting clients and expressing his opinions. Kors speaks for every American designer when he says, 'designing simple is the hardest thing in the world'.

Encouraged by his mother, an ex-Revlon model, Kors studied fashion design at the Fashion Institute of Technology in New York at the age of 18, while working as a sales assistant at Lothar's boutique on 57th Street. He quickly progressed from knowing what sold to designing his own range. The success of the collection made Kors form his own label in 1981 and he received DuPont's first American Original Award two years later. In 1995 he launched a diffusion line called Kors. He moved to Céline in late 1997, producing a successful collection in just four months, and is now creative director there.

OPPOSITE TOP **'Way to look in suits' by Lachasse: structured suit in fine Irish wool, 'brigand' collar, curvaceous lines, and hacking-jacket slits at the back, 1951.**

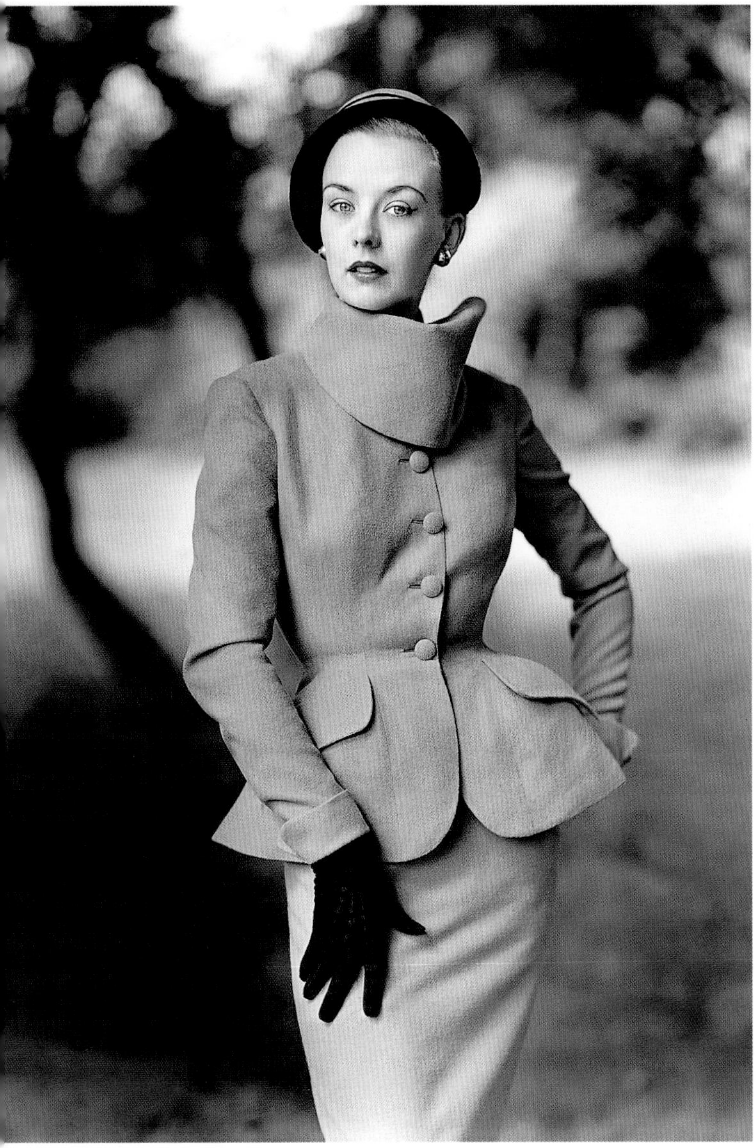

LACROIX, Christian

BORN: ARLES, FRANCE, 1951

Credited with putting a new spin on couture, and new faces in the front row, Christian Lacroix's debut in October 1987 provoked a unanimous reaction: *Vogue* talked about his irreverent spirit, while *The Sunday Times* magazine showed a photograph of 36-year-old Lacroix taking his bow with his finale bride, exclaiming on its cover: 'Vive Lacroix! There's been nothing like it for 25 years.'

Lacroix, saviour of eloquent colour and mouthwatering embroidery, studied art history and museum studies at the Sorbonne and the École du Louvre in Paris before working as an illustrator at Hermès and assistant to Guy Paulin. He spent five years at Jean Patou as chief designer of haute couture before opening his own house in 1987. The reaction verged on the orgasmic: the press were in raptures over his use of froufrou, textural mix and wonderful flair for theatricality. Lacroix scored a double whammy: he blew the cobwebs away from Paris couture and brought in the puffball skirt at the same time. Lacroix's influences – from the Queen of Arles to royal ruffles, Picasso and Cecil Beaton – reflect his love of decoration. He has designed bullfighting costumes for the world's most famous matadors. His style is full-blown rose rather than full-on sexuality. Romantic and beautiful, Lacroix's collections are examples of what occurs when a supreme colourist meets couture technique.

BELOW Lacroix's ultra-sensitive palette in lilac, rosewood and copper: boned corset, silk bustier and a splash of white silk pansies.

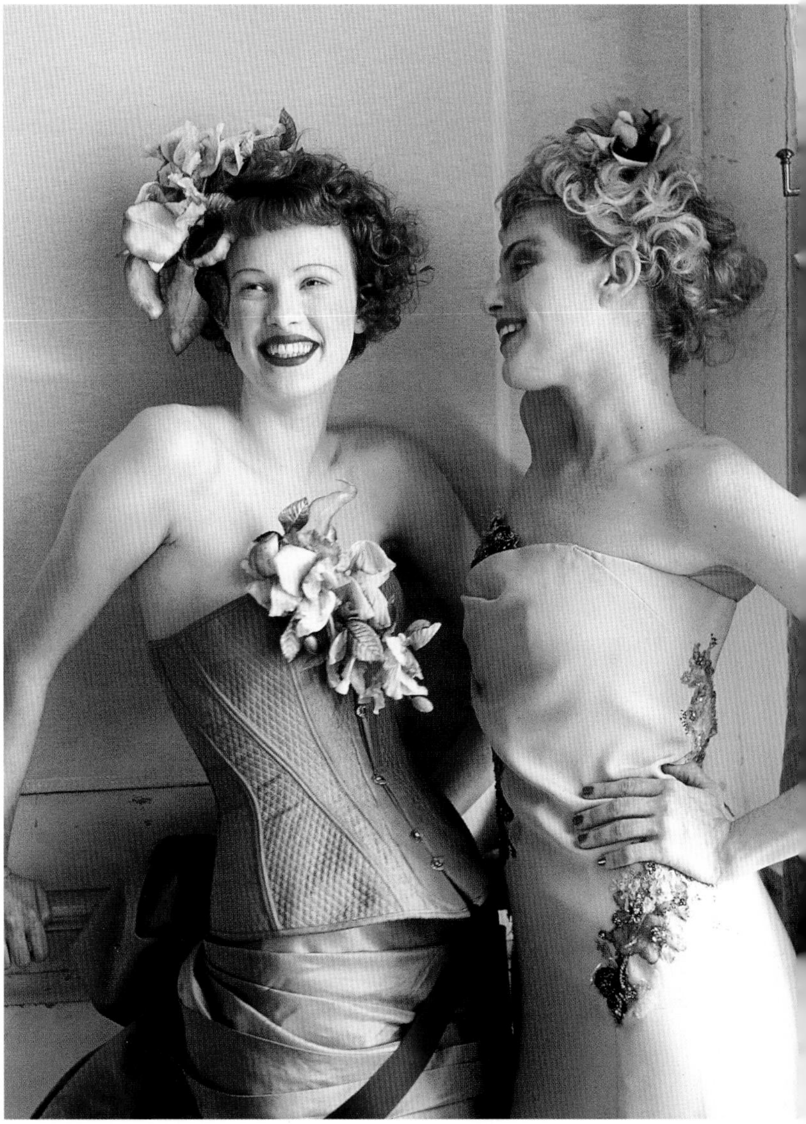

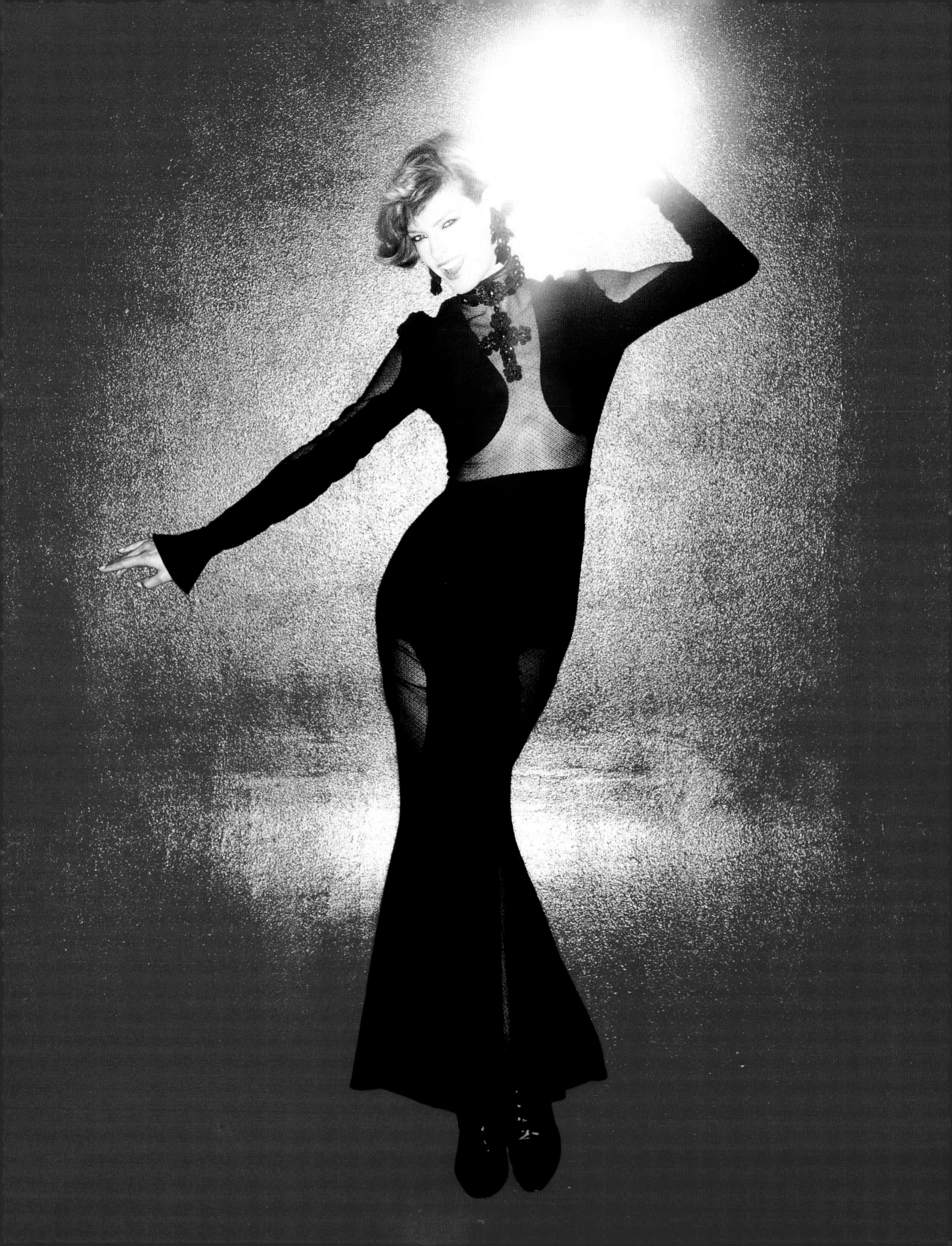

LAGERFELD, Karl

BORN: HAMBURG, GERMANY, 1938

Prolific and perceptive, Karl Lagerfeld is the designer who made Chanel a phenomenon of the 1980s and, in turn, the most significant signature of the century. No other designer could have handled it better.

When Lagerfeld arrived at Chanel in 1983 he was clearly on a roll: reinventing the Chanel suit with endless permutations, positioning the camelia on a plain white vest, putting the double 'C' insignia on motorcycle boots. He cleverly added a sporty feel, branding the puffa jacket, leggings and haversacks with the Chanel signature and thus capturing a new generation of customers.

No-one has more experience in different markets than Lagerfeld, who worked at Balmain, Patou, Chloé, Krizia, and many others. He knows how to handle fur, has a flair for irony and is also a clever fabric experimentalist: his work with the Linton Tweed mill in Carlisle included mixing Lurex with stretch and tweed with raffia. A modernist who detests museums but whose homes are reminiscent of the court of Louis XV, Lagerfeld switches styles from collection to collection in the same way that actors change character. In 1973 he told *Vogue* that 'movies are the only expression of modern thinking'. In 1983 Karl Lagerfeld made it into the most sought-after signature on the planet, becoming head designer at Chanel. Having previously worked at Chloé since the early 1960s, he returned briefly in 1993, replacing designer Martine Sitbon.

Lagerfeld's legendary fan, which has created an eclipse over his lips for years and acted as protective shield, is just one of his perennial trademarks, along with his sleek ponytail. His high-profile personality made him a natural target to hang tags on: he was called Darling Dictator, King Karl and Kaiser Karl, and was slammed as a mercenary and control freak by his competitors. Lagerfeld prefers a subtler summing-up, describing himself as an 'intelligent opportunist'.

Designing apart, Lagerfeld is an accomplished photographer and illustrator, who drew a beautiful version of *The Emperor's New Clothes*. His four lines, Chanel, Fendi, Karl Lagerfeld and

KL (his diffusion line), allow him the freedom he needs to dip into the delights of both mass-market and couture, and fly in the face of the politically correct with his extraordinary inventions using animal fur. Like Coco Chanel, Lagerfeld has a healthy attitude to plagiarism: if it's being copied, it must be good.

Still sporting his aristocratic hairdo, and with the attention span of a gnat, Lagerfeld lives on a diet of adrenaline. 'Stress? Don't name it and you don't get it,' he told American *Vogue* in 1988. 'You can say I'm a professional dilettante. What I enjoy about the job is the job.'

OPPOSITE Caught in a flash: Lagerfeld's 'transition vamp' dress, 1993, made from lace and crepe, revealing and concealing in one fell swoop.

ABOVE The ultimate in gorgeousness by Karl Lagerfeld for Chanel couture – long, lean jacket, skirt slashed to the hip, topped by a Tyrolean hat, 1990.

LANG, Helmut

BORN: VIENNA, AUSTRIA, 1956

One of the Belgian contingent of designers who put deconstruction into the fashion vocabulary, Helmut Lang established his own fashion studio in 1977. Despite having no formal training himself, he has lectured at the University of Applied Arts in Vienna.

Brought up by his grandmother in an area of mountainous tranquillity, Lang developed a taste for clean lines and linear constructions. Economy, unobtrusiveness, and a penchant for inexpensive fabrics mean that what appears to be simple is, in fact, a subtle mix of varying textures. His designs are clean and sharp – the complete antithesis of grunge. A natural futurist, he shunned the conventional catwalk show for an instinctive 'happening' on the internet.

Lang is typical of the new breed of Belgian designer: low key, anonymous and detached. A man of few words rather than master of the sound bite, he is someone who could slip into a hip restaurant without causing a ripple of swivelling heads – and his clothes are designed along the same principles. Helmut Lang – the anonymous entity with a universal label. That's the way he likes it.

LANVIN, Jeanne

BORN: BRITTANY, FRANCE, 1867
DIED: PARIS, FRANCE, 1946

Lanvin is one of the oldest established houses in Paris. Its founder, Jeanne Lanvin, served her apprenticeship as a seamstress and became a milliner, working initially from a small apartment. By 1915 Lanvin had become a byword for femininity and simplicity – and her success had made her rich. She had a house at Le Vésinet, close to Versailles and Paris, and 'was of the French designers who has made a large fortune through governing the output of styles for the young girl,' commented *Vogue* in 1915. 'She has never departed from her first conviction that modified Grecian lines are the best for the youthful figure.'

Lanvin was one of the century's first minimalists, and although she was an accomplished art collector, she did not draw direct inspiration from her paintings. Her designs relied on the use of a combination of graphic patterning, clear colours, precise positioning of details and a mix of appliqué and embroidery. Lanvin's clientele included European royalty, noted aesthetes, novelists and Hollywood stars Marlene Dietrich and Mary Pickford.

After Jeanne Lanvin's death, the house was directed by her daughter, Countess Jean de Polignac, during the 1950s, followed by Antonio del Castillo, Jules-François Crahay and, briefly, Claude Montana.

LEFT **A short, sharp exercise in how to re-work pure lace to phenomenal effect from Helmut Lang, summer 1996.**

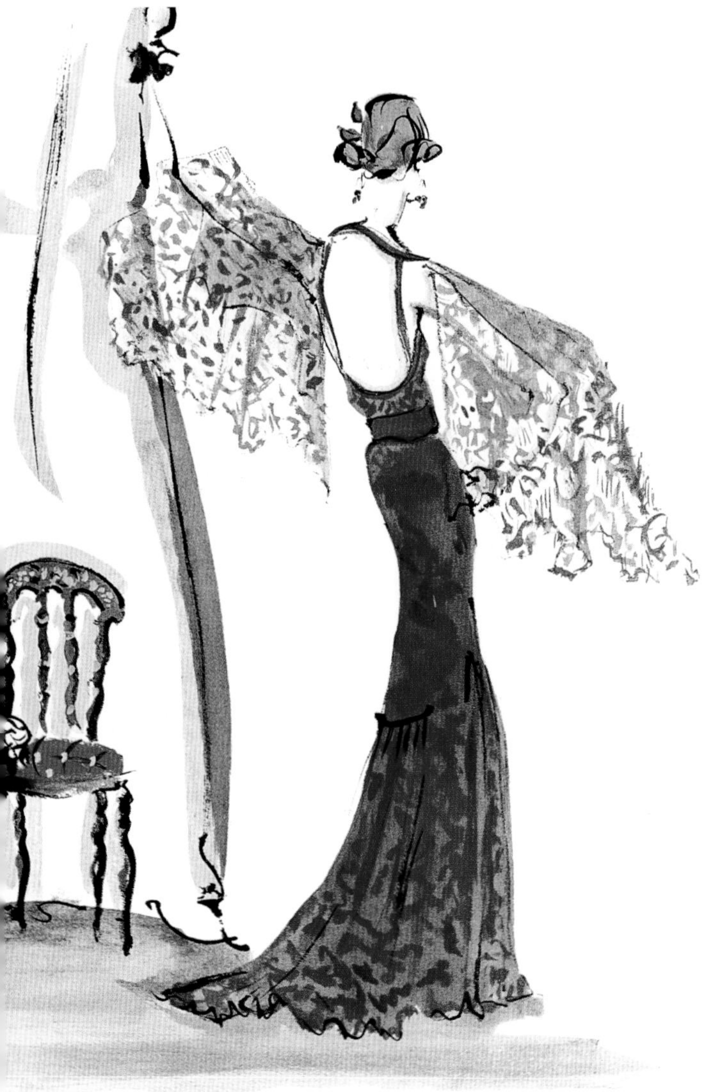

LEFT Crimson lace at Lanvin, 1936: dress 'cut slim as a reed' to balance wingspread of fine lace. Shirred panels spring low from the skirt.

LAPIDUS, Ted

BORN: PARIS, FRANCE, 1929

Son of a Russian tailor, Ted Lapidus forfeited his training in engineering to transfer his talents to fashion design. His early years were spent studying in Tokyo.

He moved to Paris in the early 1950s to open his own establishment concentrating on designing on a one-to-one basis, while exploring the possibilities of mass manufacture. He designed his clothes as a technician, concentrating his attentions as much on precision-cutting as on the design of a garment. During the 1960s he produced a safari jacket which became extremely popular. With a rounded view of the fashion industry, Lapidus has successfully kept pace with advances in both tailoring techniques and fabric technology.

LAROCHE, Guy

BORN: BORDEAUX, FRANCE, 1923
DIED: PARIS, FRANCE, 1989

When Guy Laroche burst onto the fashion scene during the mid-1950s *Vogue* commented, 'His collection puts a young kick into the traditional elegance and maturity of Paris.' By 1960 he was a mover and shaker who, together with Madame Grès, Jacques Heim, Jean Dessès, Maggy Rouff and Nina Ricci, had formed the Association des Maisons Françaises de Couture-en-Gros, a sure-fire indication that couture was, at last, being replaced by more accessible lines.

Having worked first as a milliner, and then in New York on Seventh Avenue, Laroche returned to Paris and found employment with Jean Dessès for eight years, and was talked about in the same breath as Pierre Cardin and Nina Ricci as one of the instigators of the Left-Bank look in *Vogue*'s feature, 'Half Time Score' of September 1960. 'The cloche and bob look, evocative, but new and now prevails ... narrow side-wrapped coats and suits, snuggled fur collars; head-hugging clothes; a curved slick of hair on the cheek.'

His successful apprenticeship with Dessès enabled Laroche to open his own house in 1957, where his masterful cutting and tailoring solidified his name. His early work was influenced by the architectural cutting of Cristobal Balenciaga, but he later gave this austere formality a new freshness, attracting custom from younger women. During the 1960s Laroche diversified his couture business, moving into ready to wear and specializing in reversible coats, traditional patterns and his trademark – the loose, waistless sheath. His most significant contribution at this time was for lending an almost girlish attitude to formal clothes. In the 1970s his trouser suit – a symbol for liberated women – became a wardrobe staple for women everywhere.

At the time of his death in 1989, Laroche had an extensive empire producing both couture and ready to wear. Michael Klein became couture designer in 1993, with Jean Pierre Marty in charge of ready to wear. In 1998 Laroche employed Alber Elbaz, who moved to Yves Saint Laurent's Rive Gauche line later the same year.

LAUREN, Ralph

BORN: NEW YORK, NEW YORK, USA, 1939

Ralph Lauren is the master of marketing, maestro of the seductive image, and probably the only designer who can take a period of history or slice of culture and make it totally relevant today. Lauren has taken a foray into the 1920s, a trip to Indian territory, and a safari in Africa. His greatest feat is selling Englishness to the British. His stores, which take inspiration from *Brideshead Revisited* and *The Great Gatsby*, appeal to the Ivy League graduate and low-key aristocrat. Lauren's greatest strength is his aptitude for being totally international in thinking. His shop interiors reflect stately homes: wall-to-wall mahogany, family portraits in silver frames, Navaho wraps slung nonchalantly over a sofa.

Lauren studied business science and served in the American army. He learnt all about the ins and outs of trading by doing it the hard way: selling ties. Lauren has no qualms about telling the world how he became head of a multi-million dollar empire from the shop floor. For this reason alone, he looks at the whole package rather than pondering for hours over a single outline. His flair is for themes and stories rather than seamlines and silhouettes. Lauren's advertising campaigns, shot by photographer Bruce Weber, feature Ivy League men and all-American beauties intermingling with wilting roses, thoroughbred horses and the odd wire-haired terrier. Sometimes Lauren appears himself. For him, fashion is a film set; his ultimate customer, the person who hasn't tried too hard. What he is trying to convey, he told American *Vogue* in 1992, is 'The heritage, a sense of heritage ... atmospheres of what people are and what they are doing as opposed to a Thing.'

The Lauren empire was formed in 1967 when he created his first Polo tie collection. He began with menswear and made his name by dressing Robert Redford in *The Great Gatsby* (1974); he reiterated his feel for nostalgic elegance when he dressed Diane Keaton in *Annie Hall* (1977). Lauren has won countless awards, culminating in a Lifetime Achievement Award in February 1992 from the Council of Fashion Designers of America.

Lauren's flagship store, a beautifully restored former Rhinelander mansion on Madison Avenue in New York, is an elegant combination of gentleman's club, stately sitting room and safari retreat. The shop, kitted out with polished mahogany furniture, oil paintings, lived-in leather sofas and low lighting, is the ultimate scene-setter for the look. The clothes seem to be almost incidental. Although he is the most financially successful fashion designer of modern times, Lauren admitted to *Vogue* in 1992: 'I never learned fashion, I was never a fashion person. I was a guy looking at a girl.'

ABOVE **Ralph Lauren's 'ladies man', 1992, in a lean pinstripe suit with bowler hat, silk tie and fob chain.**

OPPOSITE **Cindy Crawford in Lauren's black cashmere halterneck sheath dress, clinging to every curve, 1995.**

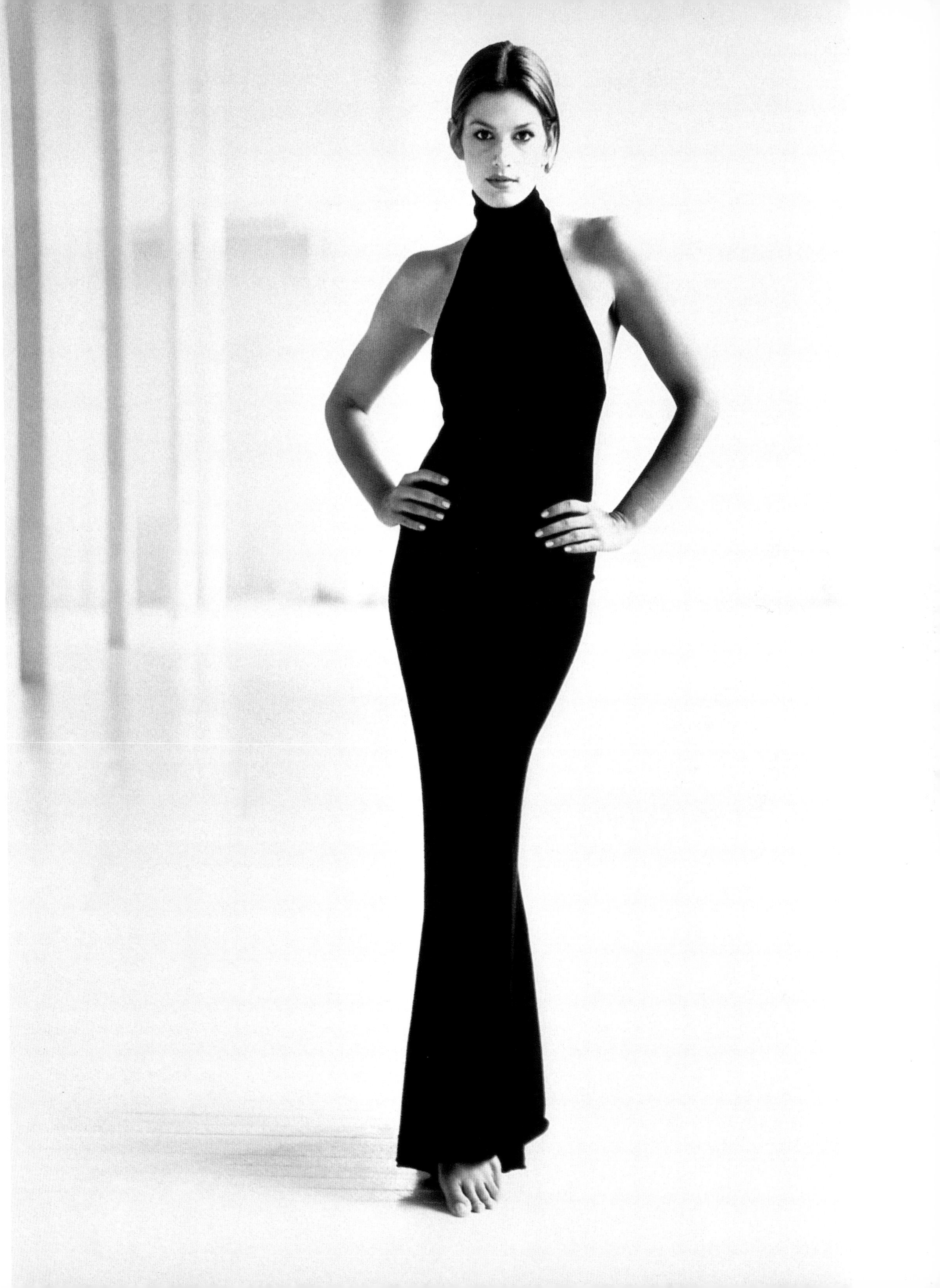

RIGHT **Lelong's 'Watteau-ish' coat of many colours from 1938, with grey panels back and front: 'sobering, flaring, daring.'**

LÉGER, Hervé

BORN: BAPAUME, FRANCE, 1957

Taking his cue from Azzedine Alaïa, Hervé Léger took the stretch, body-conscious look – which was pushed to the limit by Alaïa in the 1980s – and re-worked it for the 1990s. Léger worked at Fendi, Chanel, Lanvin, Chloé and for shoemaker Charles Jourdan before launching his own label in 1993. His clothes are instilled with the knowledge of shape and form he gathered from working at so many different fashion houses.

Léger's look takes the principles of underwear and employs them in curvaceous, clinging forms for outerwear. The comparisons with Alaïa are obvious, but Léger takes a different tack, using strips of fabric like lengths of elastic, which act as a corset. For Hervé Léger read: elasticated couture which clings to the body and helps the female form to undulate in all the right places.

LELONG, Lucien

BORN: PARIS, FRANCE, 1889
DIED: BIARRITZ, FRANCE, 1958

Son of the owner of a textile business, Lucien Lelong's debut collection was shown after the First World War. Although his contemporaries were in opposition, Lelong felt – quite rightly – that there was a market for a more diluted version of what he had already produced. The result was a diffusion line called 'Lelong Éditions'.

In the 1920s Lelong married the beautiful Princess Natalie Paley, who effectively became a walking advertisement for his latest collections. In 1925 he showed his elegant eveningwear in Paris, and at the Café de Paris in London.

Lelong was credited with preventing the disintegration of Paris couture during the war years. As president of the Chambre Syndicale de la Couture Parisienne from 1937–47, he persuaded the Germans that couture be exempt from rationing, keeping creativity alive.

Christian Dior worked with Lelong for a decade before unleashing his New Look on the world. He recalled his time working at Lelong as, 'a delightful experience – I had none of the responsibilities of putting my designs into practice on the one hand, nor the burden of an executive job on the other.'

LESAGE

FOUNDED BY ALBERT LESAGE IN 1868

France's oldest and most revered embroiderers, Lesage is the Nijinsky of the sequin, the Midas touch of craft, the glossy, priceless full stop no couture house would be without. Everyone – from Worth to Chanel to Dior – has employed the skills of France's foremost monument to elegance, the atelier that works on individual vision rather than season, where craftswomen turn couture into pieces of fine art.

Lesage's reputation has been built on its extraordinary skill in beading and its ability to construct anything a designer draws. Breathtakingly beautiful, and often working in three dimensions rather than on a flat surface, some of the most notable Lesage inventions include a sizzling lamé bow and a celebration of the Fabergé egg. They have also created a trompe l'oeil shower for Karl Lagerfeld, a Byzantine breastplate for Christian Lacroix, an angular Picasso profile for Yves Saint Laurent, and a glittering bunch of succulent sequinned grapes and spiked leaves, which hung from the shoulder of an Yves Saint Laurent satin jacket and was described by *Vogue* in 1988 simply as, 'A vintage season of Lesage embroidery.'

LESTER, Charles & Patricia

Founded by Charles and Patricia Lester in 1964

Makers of Fortuny-esque dresses, Charles and Patricia Lester have forged a niche in perpendicular pleating. Their dresses sell in Japan, Italy and America, and customers range from the Duchess of Kent to Barbra Streisand – with Shakira Caine and Bette Midler in between. Using a mix of silk-screen printing techniques and permanent pleating, the Lester look is opulent and exotic, and spans everything from evening dresses to cushions to waistcoats.

Charles was originally a textile physicist, while Patricia – with no formal training – began designing in 1964 and in June 1988 was appointed a MBE. Working from their studio on the River Usk in Wales, the Lesters use a mixture of hand-dyeing, tie-dyeing, batik and silk-screen printing to create a look that is richly coloured with an air of fluidity.

LIBERTY

Founded by Arthur Lasenby Liberty in 1875

Over a century after its inception, Liberty, Rossetti and the Pre-Raphaelite movement still go hand in hand. Founded as a fabric and clothing emporium to extol the aesthetic movement, Liberty was instrumental in liberating women from corsetry. The store was famous for importing fabrics and re-dyeing them in exotic colours; it was also a popular source of inspiration for Paris couturiers.

Although Liberty's influences were firmly rooted in the Greek, Roman and Medieval period when clothing was at its most simple, its style always centred on opulence and used fabrics such as devoré velvets and silk satin. Curiously, while the space race gained momentum in the 1960s, Liberty enjoyed a renaissance, with an influx of young designers and psychedelic colours. Spiritual home to Jean Muir and haven for legions of customers, who rate it as the most beautiful store in the world, Liberty is undergoing a revamp to coincide with the millennium.

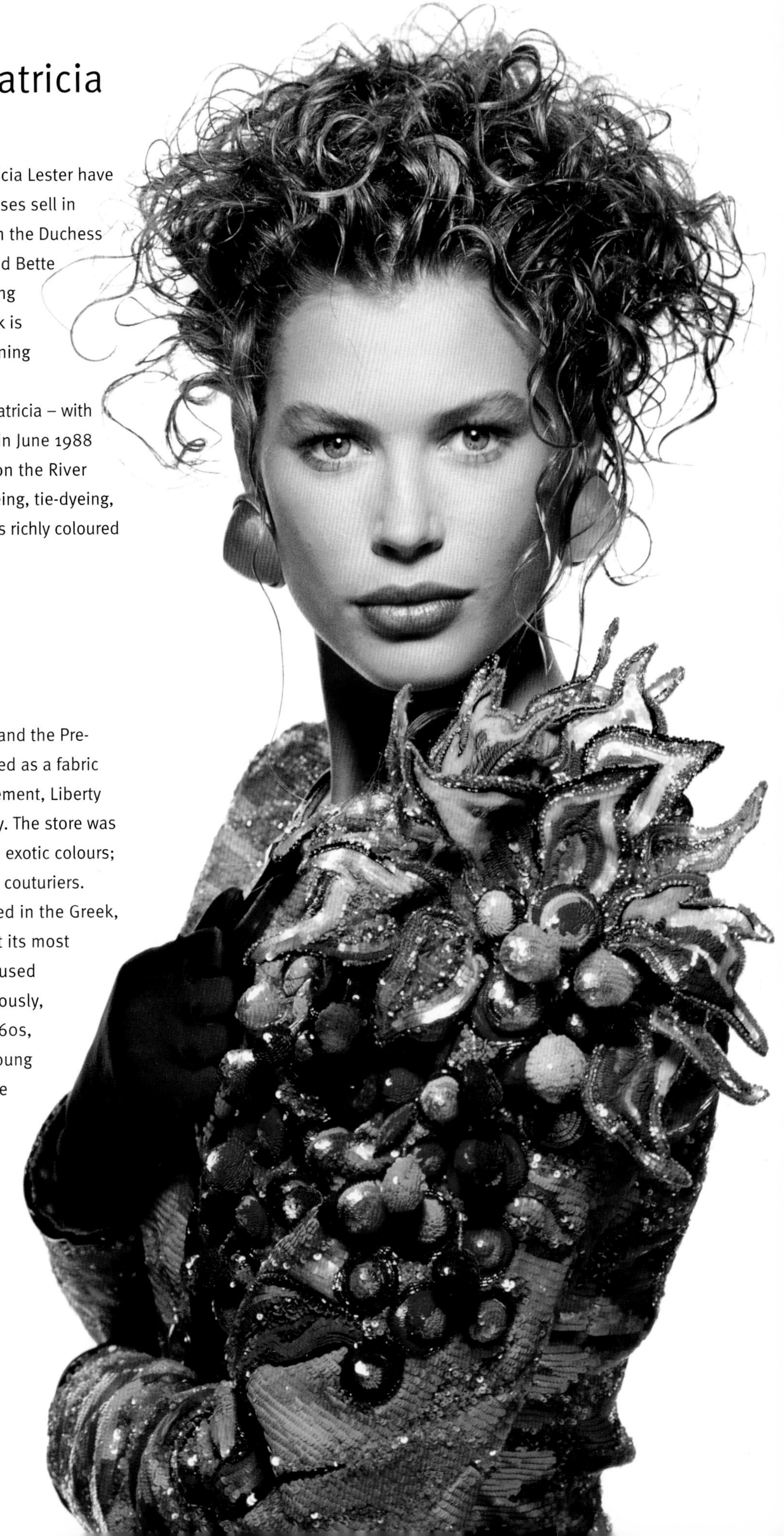

RIGHT A vintage season for Lesage: bunches of glossy grapes in three dimensions, sprouting leaves on an Yves Saint Laurent jacket, 1988.

LOEWE

FOUNDED BY ENRIQUE LOEWE IN 1846

Famous for its heritage of impeccable craftsmanship and soft leathers, Loewe is the most recent luxury goods company to undergo a revamp. The Spanish company – based in Madrid with branches around the world – appointed Narciso Rodriguez as its design director in 1997. Rodriguez, who created Carolyn Bessette Kennedy's wedding dress in 1996, felt the contract was a meeting of minds: 'Loewe's Latin and I'm Latin,' he said succinctly. Rodriguez, who was brought up in New York but is of Spanish descent, is used to cross-cultural referencing. He has continued to nurture the Loewe label, directing it beyond accessories and into a collection which contains luxurious references and spicy colouring.

LOUBOUTIN, Christian

BORN: PARIS, FRANCE, 1963

A French shoemaker of considerable note with a long line of celebrity clients, including Inès de la Fressange, Princess Caroline of Monaco and Catherine Deneuve, Christian Louboutin works in the tradition of his hero, shoe designer Roger Vivier. Colourful and beautiful – particularly when they are embroidered – Louboutin shoes are not particularly practical or simple, veering instead towards the fantastical.

LOUISEBOULANGER

FOUNDED BY LOUISE BOULANGER IN 1927

Louise Boulanger started out as a 13-year-old apprentice before becoming a designer at the house of Chéruit, eventually opening Louiseboulanger, her own business, in 1927. She made regular appearances in *Vogue*, often alongside her contemporaries – Madeleine Vionnet, Edward Molyneux, Coco Chanel and later, Elsa Schiaparelli. Louiseboulanger's skill was in switching from tailoring to eveningwear, from day dresses to cocktail ensembles. As the decades progressed, Louiseboulanger retained the ability to move on, never sticking to one single style, but adapting to fluctuating hemlines and radical shifts in taste. She was one of the first designers to recognize the potential of evening wraps, was an expert in little black dresses and could make fluid evening gowns comparable only to Vionnet's. A vastly underrated designer, Louiseboulanger was a *tour de force* and regular fixture on *Vogue*'s fashion pages for 20 years.

ABOVE '**Black returns to Chic, via Paris': Louiseboulanger's chiffon evening wraps, eloquently embroidered. Right, black crepe Romain dress, 1926.**

LUCAS, Otto

BORN: GERMANY, 1903
DIED: BELGIUM, 1971

London's most stylish hatmaker during the 1950s, Otto Lucas opened his business in 1932, and directed the shape of British millinery from his salon in central London. Presiding over an enormous workroom, Lucas's precise attention to detail, wonderful proportions and expertise at handling a variety of fabrics and multitude of styles made him one of the key players during the decade when accessories were imperative to the total look. Tragically, he was killed in a plane crash.

Working for Britain's most prolific milliner was not all sweetness and light: Lucas was described by one ex-employee – who did not wish to speak ill of the deceased – as having 'wonderful style – but hell to work for'.

McCARDELL, Claire

BORN: FREDERICK, MARYLAND, USA, 1905
DIED: NEW YORK, NEW YORK, USA, 1958

The post-Second World War precursor to Donna Karan, Calvin Klein, Ralph Lauren and a coterie of American classicists, Claire McCardell is the mother of American sportswear. In *Vogue* in 1941 she was described as, 'The typical American girl – whom you never saw but read about in print.'

McCardell's penchant for pattern cutting and dressing up began in her childhood, and she eventually progressed to re-modelling clothes with the use of a small sewing machine. She graduated from Hood College in Maryland, and later attended Parson's School of Design in New York, living at the Three Arts Club – a home and club for women in the arts. McCardell was then transferred to the Paris branch of Parson's, situated in the place des Vosges. 'I was learning important things all the time; the way clothes worked, the way they felt, where they fastened,' she reflected later of her invaluable year in the fashion capital. She returned to New York to complete her final year in 1928. Her first job was as an illustrator with Emmet Joyce, for which she received the princely sum of $20 per week. From there, McCardell progressed to designing knitwear, and eventually scouring rival stores for a company called Robert Turk. When Turk switched jobs he took McCardell with him; when he drowned in a tragic accident, she became head designer. Although McCardell did the designer rounds – travelling to Paris, making sketches and interpreting various styles – she knew there was a market for real Americanism.

The turning point came when McCardell made an Algerian-style evening dress with a sportswear slant to wear to the Beaux-Arts Ball. The shorter version she'd made for herself prompted compliments and naturally found its way into the collection. This invention kick-started the rest of her range – an instinctive line of revolutionary, pragmatic designs.

McCardell's creations were always based on logical thought rather than playing with proportion. She invented the Pop-over, a sturdy denim wraparound smock, which became an American classic; she used heavy-duty linen to make feminine versions of male workwear; jersey exercise suits; silk playsuits. Every pocket

RIGHT **Claire McCardell's effortless, modern playsuit of 1953, buttoning at the front, tied at the waist, and worn with a beret. Perfect for beach bathing.**

placement, diameter of strap, twin stitching or length of a skirt had a reason, otherwise it wouldn't be there. Her consummate flair was for simplicity and her approach was based on the belief that necessity is the mother of invention. McCardell was the personification of the word 'utility'. In 1987 the Fashion Institute of Technology in New York staged an exhibition celebrating the work of Madeleine Vionnet, Rei Kawakubo and Claire McCardell, three women with differing styles, bound together by a common thread of intelligence.

McCARTNEY, Stella

BORN: LONDON, ENGLAND, 1972

Appointed design director of Chloé in 1997 to a chorus of criticism and accusations of 'nepotism' – her father, Paul, wrote the most mesmerizing songs of the century – Stella McCartney has proved she can deliver the goods, and that she is much more than a PR puppet. She has put a fresh new slant on the Chloé label, and her collections have been rapturously received. More importantly, customers are putting their money where their mouths are: sales of Chloé have shot up by 500 per cent.

McCartney was educated at a comprehensive school in Sussex; she studied fashion at London's Central Saint Martins College of Art and Design, and worked at Christian Lacroix and Betty Jackson before securing the position at Chloé. Like her mother, Linda, who pioneered vegetarianism, faced the wrath of Beatles' fans and smiled in the face of breast cancer, it will take more than the odd poison arrow to knock McCartney off kilter.

RIGHT What Stella McCartney does best: simple shifts – in this case, lace-panelled and secured with wide straps, 1997. Bright tights optional.

'I had a lot of those stupid millennium questions – but why would I do a white number or a 2001 theme?' she told *Vogue* in 1999. 'What the next millennium is about, for me, is confidence.'

MACDONALD, Julien

BORN: METHYR TYDFIL, WALES, 1974

A clever, inventive knitwear designer, who was born in Wales and works in London, Julien Macdonald was spotted by Karl Lagerfeld, who employed him almost as soon as he left London's Royal College of Art in 1996. MacDonald is an experimentalist – a bold designer who is more than happy to dip his toe into unchartered waters. He mixes crocheting with conventional knitting, sparkle with stretch, unidentified flying objects – namely sweet wrappers, real gold and crystals – with pure new wool. His speciality is dresses which leave areas of flesh on show, effectively revealing and concealing at the same time. More suited to one-offs than the constraints of commercial enterprise, MacDonald successfully pushes the boundaries – lifting knitwear out of its more conventional sphere. He currently sells in the USA, Tokyo and Paris, and his celebrity clients range from Nicole Kidman to Madonna.

McFADDEN, Mary

BORN: NEW YORK, NEW YORK, USA, 1938

Instantly recognizable by her sharp black haircut and existentialist looks, Mary McFadden attended the École Lubec in Paris during the 1950s, before studying fashion at the Traphagen School of Design and Sociology in New York. By the time she decided to settle on the fashion industry she already had various work experiences: director of public relations at Dior, merchandizing for South African *Vogue*, political columnist and jewellery designer. In addition, she had founded a sculpture workshop in Rhodesia and had an acute knowledge of classical art and ancient civilization.

McFadden's experience of cross cultures and diverse social types has meant that her clothes have surprising elements – simple lines and exotic prints. She readily admits she's more into fabric than fashion. Her business kicked off in 1973 when Geraldine Stutz, then president of New York store Henri Bendel, encouraged her to explore the medium of fashion. The result: a white strapless column for Jacqueline Onassis. She has also dressed Diana Vreeland, Ethel Kennedy and Evelyn Lauder.

MACKIE, Bob

Born: Los Angeles, California, USA, 1940

Theatrical, camp and unashamedly over the top, Bob Mackie is best known for his sequinned creations worn at the Oscars, on videos and at every appropriate photo opportunity by singer-turned-actress, Cher. Mackie's forte is turning women into showgirl parodies, Caesar's Palace extras and glossy exotic insects. His natural habitat is Las Vegas; his favourite mediums are feathers, sequins and tantalizing sheers. In 1990 Mackie tried his hand at American folk art, drawing inspiration from what he described to *The New York Times* as 'the men and women that forged the wilderness'. The uninitiated expected homespun values but the result was typically flamboyant: *Custer's Last Stand* crossed with *La Cage Au Folles*.

Mackie became known in the USA for his work with comedienne Carol Burnett. He was responsible for her on-set wardrobe – which included relatively quiet suits and character costumes – for over a decade. When Mackie entered the ready-to-wear market, his name was already associated with glitz. He did not disappoint, and his shows gave a taste of showmanship to the sedate proceedings. Mackie has the ability to produce quiet suits, but his forte will always be more Las Vegas than Sunset Boulevard. As a result, his customers are women who want to make an effect. Speaking to *People* magazine in 1998, Chastity Bono, daughter of Cher, recalled: 'She didn't pick me up in Bob Mackie gowns or anything, but she didn't look like June Cleaver either.'

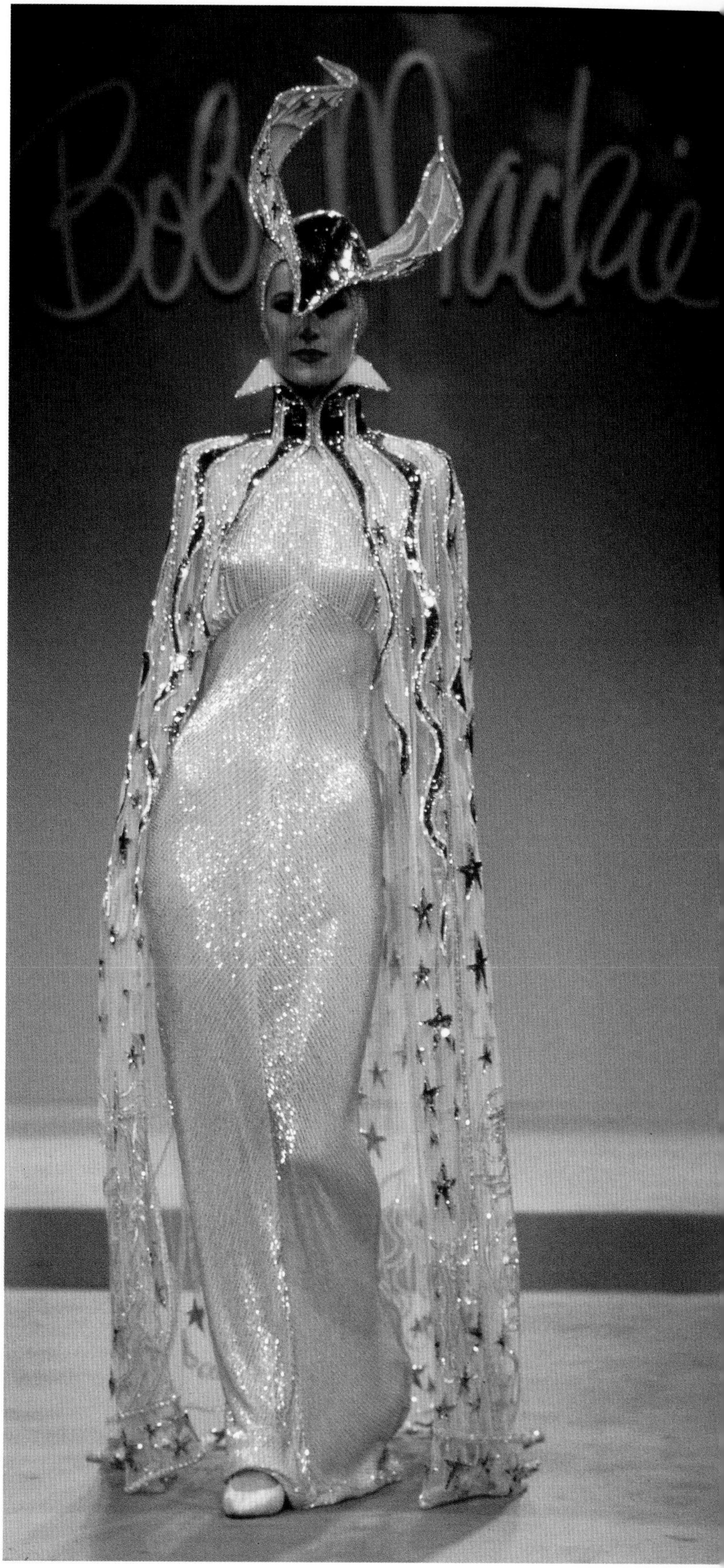
Bob Mackie

RIGHT **Viva Las Vegas: Bob Mackie's unmistakable glamour: head-to-toe sequins, swirling headdress and reflections in all directions, 1989.**

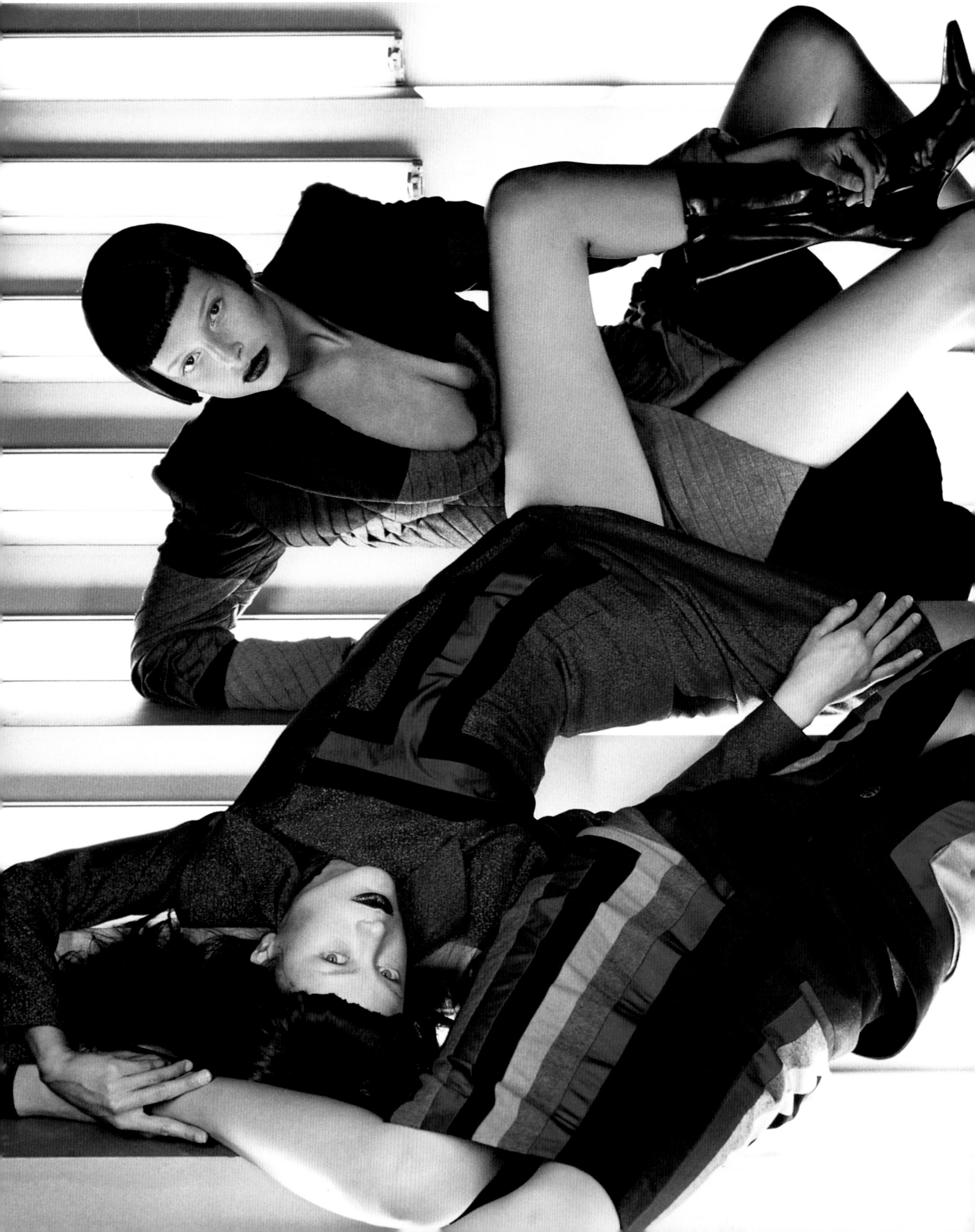

McQUEEN, Alexander

Born: London, England, 1969

The self-styled bad boy of Paris couture, Alexander McQueen is the son of a taxi driver who found himself, virtually overnight, in the hot seat at Givenchy. McQueen was discovered by *Vogue* stylist Isabella Blow, who was sitting in the audience at his MA show. She took the collection, wore it in a *Vogue* shoot in November 1992, and relentlessly promoted him. It was Blow who persuaded McQueen to change his name from Lee to the more exotic-sounding Alexander.

McQueen is brilliant at self-publicity and causing a controversy; much has been made of his working-class roots, cockney accent and outspoken opinions. Pre-Central Saint Martins School of Art and Design, London, McQueen was already adept in the technical aspects of making clothes. His career began at the Savile Row tailor Anderson & Sheppard. McQueen moved to Kohji Tatsuno as a pattern-cutter and flew to Milan on a whim, eventually securing a position with Romeo Gigli before returning to London to do an MA.

On graduating, he formed his own line and then had a hit: his bumster trousers – a style which exposed the upper part of the posterior (more commonly seen on building sites) – caused a minor sensation and made his name. He received the British Designer of the Year Award in 1996 and, when John Galliano moved from Givenchy to Christian Dior, McQueen filled the position. He swept into Paris, slating everyone in his wake, including Vivienne Westwood and John Galliano. Hubert de Givenchy – the founder of the house and one of the most respected designers of the century – was dismissed as irrelevant by McQueen.

Ironically, McQueen's first collection for Givenchy was universally panned. At least he had the grace to admit it himself. 'I know it was crap,' he told American *Vogue* in October 1997 with typical candour, vowing to make amends with the next collection. McQueen is one of the few Central Saint Martins' graduates with real technical ability and a Savile Row training. His triumphs include Kate Winslet's wedding dress in 1999. McQueen's shows are always sensational, but his collections blow hot and cold. 'If you want a starving Ethiopian on a jacket, then come to McQueen in London,' he told *Vogue* in 1997. 'If you want luxury, come to Givenchy. I do both. I'm a fashion schizophrenic.'

LEFT Savile Row-trained McQueen uses a blend of angles, curves and subtle colour to make suits that are anything but straight, 1998.

MAINBOCHER

BORN: CHICAGO, ILLINOIS, USA, 1890
DIED: NEW YORK, NEW YORK, USA, 1976

Mainbocher was the American who took Paris by storm in 1929 and returned, triumphant, to the USA having been editor at French *Vogue*, established his own couture house and designed the Duchess of Windsor's trousseau. Mainbocher's grounding served him well for his new couture house in New York: several years as editor of French *Vogue* taught him the importance of publicity, as well as a remarkable ability to foresee exactly which direction fashion was going. He was, in effect, a detached designer with a flair for publicity and an antennae for style.

Born Main Rousseau Bocher, he attended the Chicago Academy of Fine Arts, and had various occupations – including illustrator and writer – before leaving *Vogue* to set up his own

BELOW 'The modern full dress' at Mainbocher: left, crepe dress, with fringed scarf; right, white crepe gown with 'cock feather' appliqué, 1932.

OPPOSITE 'The easiest city look' – perennial white shirt, cotton jersey vest top, gaberdine trousers and body bag – Martin Margiela for Hermès, 1999.

house. From the outset, Mainbocher established himself as a name that was synonymous with luxury and exclusivity. He made several dresses for the Duchess of Windsor – including her bias-cut wedding dress – thus satisfying her dual needs for French style and American patronage. Other notable clients included the Vanderbilts and socialite C Z Guest. Curiously, for a designer with inside knowledge of how the fashion industry, works, Mainbocher had no compulsion to exploit his name. He remained a couture designer, with a slight concession to ready to wear, until the end.

MARGIELA, Martin

BORN: LOUVAIN, BELGIUM, 1957

A key member of the Belgian avant-garde and former assistant to Jean Paul Gaultier, Martin Margiela introduced the word 'deconstruction' into the fashion vocabulary, and made the notion of the designer interview passé. Margiela is so low profile that he's virtually invisible. Initially training as a fine artist, he became a stylist, and then design assistant to Gaultier in 1985; he showed his first collection in 1988. Margiela's talent is for pushing the boundaries: his reference points are punk, medieval detail and recycling old clothes (T-shirts made out of used shopping bags, sweaters constructed out of socks). His approach to where he holds his shows is equally unconventional, with collections shown in both a cemetery and a disintegrating fire station.

Margiela uses colour in conjunction with what it means to people; he totally understands the subliminal messages given out by red as opposed to black. In 1997 he was appointed to design Hermès' ready-to-wear collection – an inspired choice to attract the fashion literate and reinvigorate the label. In 1999 he turned his talents to designing for the French catalogue *3Suisses* – along with Karl Lagerfeld, Thierry Mugler and his former boss, Jean Paul Gaultier. Although his work is widely viewed as an art form, Margiela does not put fashion on a pedestal: 'Fashion is a craft, a technical know-how and not, in our opinion, an art form,' he told the *Guardian*. 'Each world shares an expression through very divergent media processes.'

MATSUDA, Mitsuhiro

BORN: TOKYO, JAPAN, 1934

Mitsuhiro Matsuda travelled to Paris with his contemporary, Kenzo, in the 1960s. Tellingly, he returned to Japan while Kenzo remained. The designs say it all: Matsuda has retained the Japanese aesthetic for non-conformist cutting.

Matsuda started his career as a designer of ready to wear, then formed his own company, Nicole Limited. He eventually launched his own line in 1987. Matsuda's influences are diverse: from Pre-Raphaelite paintings to the Arts and Crafts movement. His clothes contain lush embroidery, medieval construction and subliminal references to jazz. Like Romeo Gigli, his collections have a medieval touch which appeals to renaissance women.

MAXMARA

FOUNDED BY ACHILLE MARAMOTTI IN 1951

Italy's leading ready-to-wear company, MaxMara, was founded by Achille Maramotti, who began with a miniscule capsule collection of one coat and two suits. This eventually metamorphosed into an international powerhouse with five manufacturing companies. The MaxMara empire encompasses 16 labels, which include MaxMara, Sportmax and Marella.

The quality of MaxMara's collections is always impeccable. Many famous designers have contributed to the label, including Karl Lagerfeld, Jean-Charles de Castelbajac, Emmanuelle Khanh and more recently Guy Paulin and Dolce et Gabbana. Photographers who have added to the company's corporate image and international cachet include *Vogue* contributors Peter Lindberg, Arthur Elgort and Paolo Roversi.

MARNI

FOUNDED BY CONSUELO CASTIGLIONI IN 1992

Described as bohemian, sensory and superluxe, the Marni label treads a fine line between precise detail and considered disarray.

Swiss-born Consuelo married Gianni Castiglioni, president of Ciwi furs, a branch of Fendi's family tree, when she was 25 years old. After having two children, Castiglioni became a fashion consultant for the company. She progressed to produce her own line, unveiling her first collection of immaculate leathers in 1992 and going on to use natural fabrics – thus creating the look that has personified the late 1990s: antique chic. Her expertise lies in knowing how to encapsulate the twin Italian strengths of gorgeous fabrics and a fabulous finish. In March 1999 she created a new collection of accessories.

MISSONI

FOUNDED BY OTTAVIO AND ROSITA MISSONI IN 1953

The company founded by Ottavio and Rosita Missoni produces fine yarns, ripples of colour and, above all, fantastic knitwear. No-one knows how to knit like the Italians, and Missoni knitwear is finely tuned, with a background of supreme technology. Missoni have managed to make their yarns look and feel like precious antiques, even though they are totally modern in concept. The Missonis have always followed their own line – a mixture of checks, spots and, as we go into the millennium, multiple patterns.

MIYAKE, Issey

BORN: HIROSHIMA, JAPAN, 1938

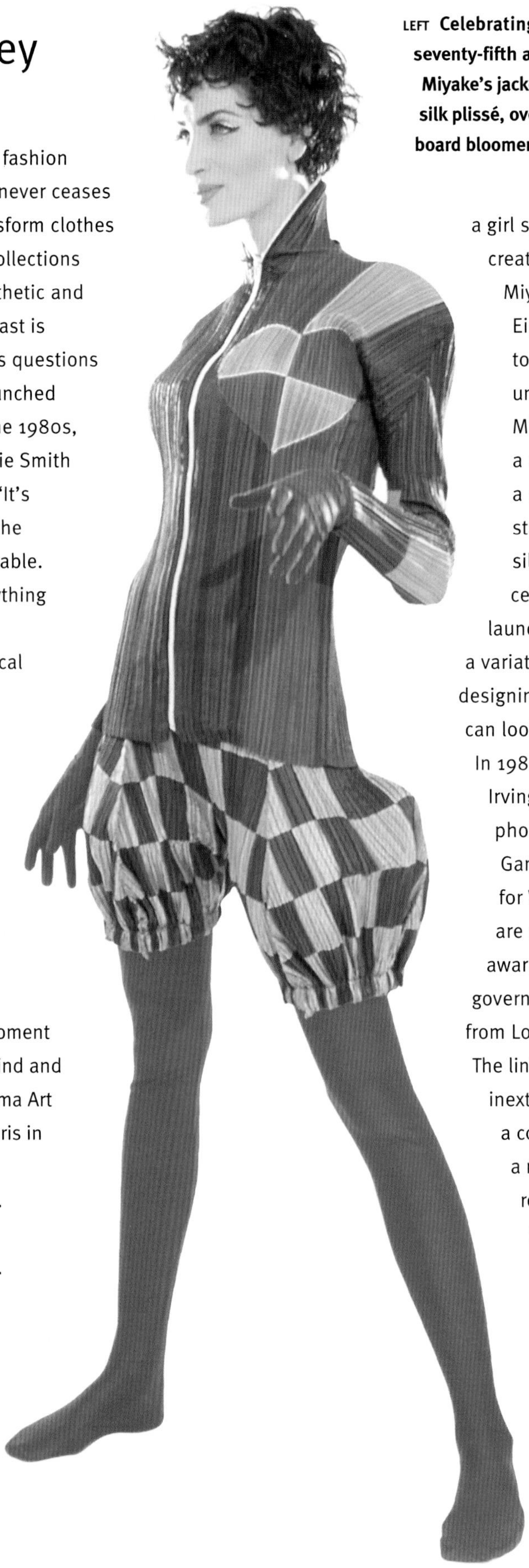

LEFT **Celebrating *Vogue*'s seventy-fifth anniversary, Miyake's jacket of pewter silk plissé, over chequer-board bloomers, 1991.**

OPPOSITE **Showing how structure should be handled: Issey Miyake's sculptured coat with wind hood to combat the outside elements, 1986.**

Issey Miyake thinks form before fashion and concept before clothes. He never ceases to amaze with his ability to transform clothes into organic objects. Miyake's collections have been called monastic, aesthetic and completely unfathomable. This last is probably because Miyake always questions rather than follows: when he launched his 'Permanente' collection in the 1980s, the Oscar-winning actress Maggie Smith enthused in *The Sunday Times*, 'It's an amusing idea and above all the clothes are fantastically comfortable. They are so easy you can do anything in them. I always wear them for rehearsals because their theatrical quality helps.'

Miyake was 7 years old when he witnessed the atom bomb which killed 200,000 of Hiroshima's inhabitants and reduced two-thirds of the city to ashes. Three years later he developed osteomyelitis, a disease of the bone marrow; his mother died shortly afterwards. He put the moment of mass-destruction out of his mind and became a graphics student at Tama Art University in Tokyo, moving to Paris in the 1960s and working with Guy Laroche and Hubert de Givenchy. Miyake then moved to New York and worked with Geoffrey Beene.

When he returned to Tokyo in 1970, Japan had undergone a sea change. Kimonos and Western shapes had interbred – it was the perfect moment to forge a new direction. His first collection had a girl systematically stripping off her Miyake creation. The show caused a scandal and Miyake became an overnight sensation. Eight years before Comme des Garçons took Paris by storm, Miyake showed his unconventional collection in Paris.

Miyake's clothes never start from a sketch, but from scratch – a piece of fabric, a notion of movement. In the 1980s he staged a Bodywork exhibition with black silicon models – some suspended from the ceiling, others submerged in darkness. He launched his collection for men in 1982, wearing a variation on a shirt-jacket, which he had been designing since 1975: 'Men who follow fashion can look ridiculous,' he told *Vogue*.

In 1988 Miyake collaborated with photographer Irving Penn to produce a book of startling photographs. He designed the Olympic Games outfits for Lithuania and vestments for Winchester cathedral in 1992. Accolades are numerous: the following year Miyake was awarded the Légion d'honneur by the French government, followed by an honorary doctorate from London's Royal College of Art.

The link between Issey Miyake and art is inextricable. All his collections – from 'Windcoat', a collection of outerwear to 'Pleats Please', a range of polyester pieces – contain aesthetic reference points. His customers are creative thinkers; his collections celebrations of pliable human sculpture. As guest artist Yasumasa Morimura commented, 'Miyake questions, "Why?" and "Wait a minute!" about his own clothing designs. This "?" is a source of creative energy. "Why?" has the power to shake one's thoughts. This is called an *étonnement*; the French word for shaking, disturbance, or astonishment.'

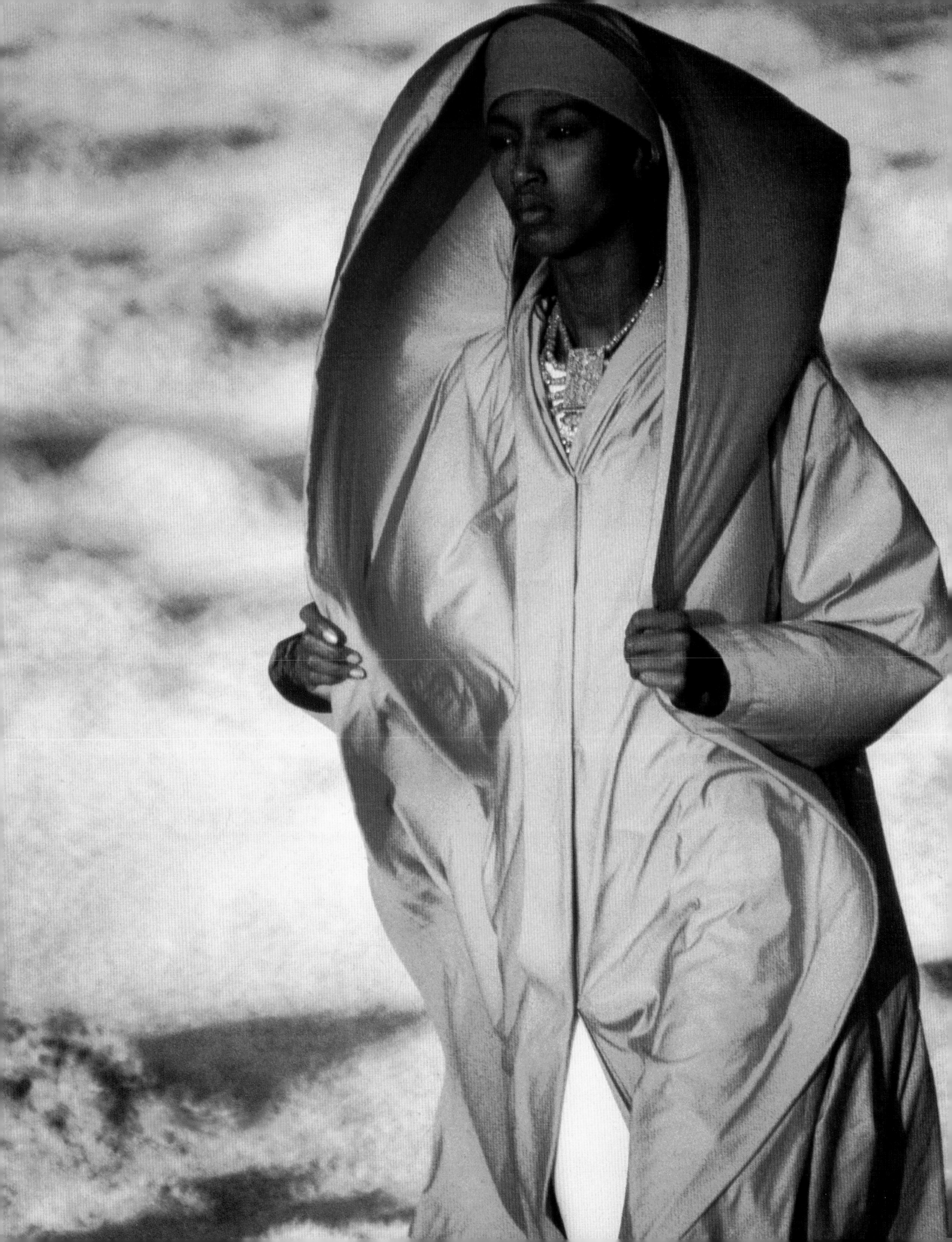

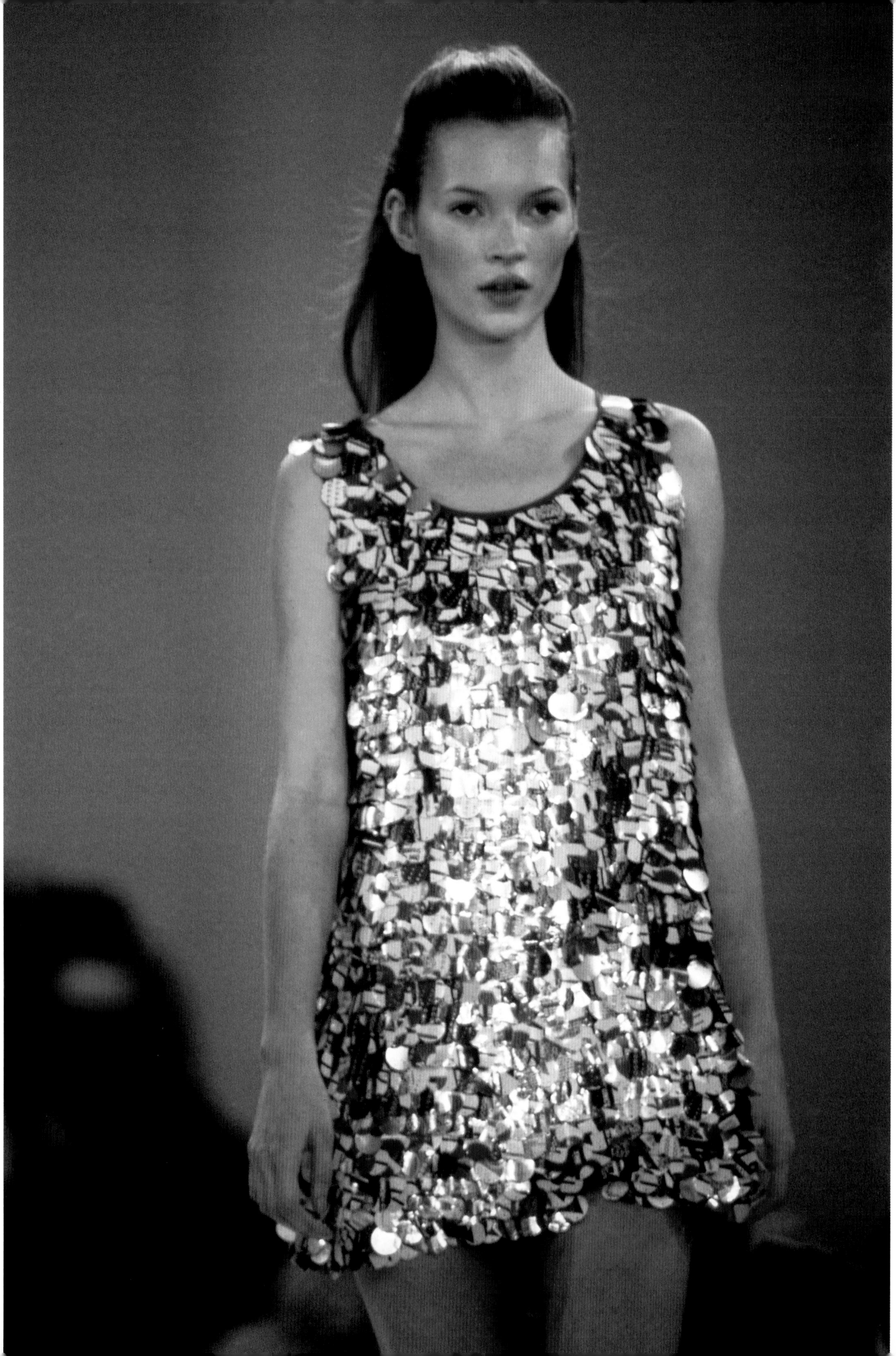

OPPOSITE Isaac Mizrahi's short, shimmering, multicoloured shift, worn by Kate Moss on the catwalk and shown in *Vogue*'s fashion supplement of 1994.

MIZRAHI, Isaac

BORN: NEW YORK, NEW YORK, USA, 1961

Isaac Mizrahi arrived on the fashion scene in 1989 to a flurry of praise, a flash of sequins and a headline that called him a 'shooting star'. Then 27, Mizrahi had an exuberant sense of colour, an infectious energy, and a youthful eye with an edited grown-up outlook. His earliest design influences stemmed from his mother's all-American wardrobe, which included clothing from Halston, Geoffrey Beene, Claire McCardle and Norman Norell. 'The American ethos is very simple, very underdone, not over-constructed,' he said, while sending immaculate cashmere sweaters and sparkle-knit shifts down the catwalk. 'I don't really want to do clothes for 18 year olds. They look best in jeans and funny little things they put together themselves.'

Mizrahi graduated from Parsons School of Design in New York in 1982. He then worked for Perry Ellis and Calvin Klein before forming his company in 1992. Three years later, *Unzipped* was launched at the Cannes film festival. The film was a fascinating, fly-on-the-wall documentary which followed an often tortured Mizrahi as he designed his autumn/winter collection, dreamed up an arresting catwalk show, and interacted with supermodels including Naomi Campbell and Cindy Crawford. Such a revealing insight served both to heighten Mizrahi's profile and leave him exposed at the same time – he was the first designer to be caught on camera in the process of being crushed by the critics.

Despite the success of his subsequent collections, by 1998 Mizrahi was a fashion casualty; when his studio closed it was considered a sufficiently newsworthy event to make the front page of *The New York Times*. For Mizrahi, the sadness was tinged with a sense of relief: at least the photograph was a slimline one. His parting shot – a quote about fashion getting tougher – allowed him to concentrate on what he enjoys doing most: airing his opinions with self-deprecating wit, and nurturing his status as a 'personality'. Mizrahi is a regular contributor to American *Vogue*; he also writes for various other publications and makes numerous television appearances.

MODEL, Philippe

BORN: SENS, FRANCE, 1956

Milliner and shoe designer, Philippe Model grew up in the French countryside. His father ran a leather tannery and he spent his childhood reworking leather offcuts into feasible accessories. At the age of 20, the department store Galléries Lafayette promoted a military cap designed by Model, which proved to be a bestseller and launched him as a designer. Model then embarked on a career in which his contemporaries were to present him with an award for Best Craftsman in France. He became a distinguished maker of quirky and covetable accessories, designing under his own name and also that of Michel Perry. Model established his own company in 1981 and by 1993 his designs were distributed to over 200 stores throughout the world, including three of his own shops in Paris.

He has worked with Jean Paul Gaultier, Claude Montana, Issey Miyake and Thierry Mugler, and has accessorized the elegant outfits of a series of French movie stars, as well as Princess Caroline of Monaco.

Unusually, Model is known equally for his millinery and his footwear – neat, elasticated shoes formed from stretch material which have been widely copied. Additional lines include men's knitwear, perfume, interior design and costumes and shoes for opera, one of Model's passions.

MOLINARI, Anna

BORN: CAPRI, ITALY, 1948

Anna Molinari, the designer behind Blumarine, began the business in collaboration with her husband in 1977. Initially concentrating on knitwear, Molinari won the Designer of the Year Award in 1980. In 1990 the company, based in Italy, expanded abroad to Spain, Austria, Paris and Japan. The Anna Molinari label, known for its brilliant use of colour, is now designed by Molinari's daughter, but the Blumarine line, designed by Molinari herself, continues to personify the designer's signature style of creating sexy glamorous clothes. Believing that every woman has a dual fashion personality, known as the virgin/whore complex, Molinari has striven to incorporate both in her collections, attracting a following of ultra-feminine customers in the process. As the millennium approaches, Blumarine's bestseller is a fitted cardigan edged with real fur.

MOLYNEUX,
Captain Edward

BORN: LONDON, ENGLAND, 1891
DIED: LONDON, ENGLAND, 1974

A respected, immaculately dressed couturier of Irish descent, Edward Molyneux's strength was his sense of propriety and understanding of wearability. Described by Pierre Balmain, an ex-employee, in his autobiography, *My Years and Seasons* (1964) as an 'elegant, aloof Englishman who held the fashion world in the palm of his hand during the 1930s', *Vogue* put it more succinctly: 'His is the suit that lives forever.'

Molyneux's clients encompassed diplomatic and court circles, and during the 1920s and 1930s no social occasion was complete without a Molyneux outfit making an appearance. The epitome of simplicity, the clothes were constructed on the perennial ideals of perfection and taste. Molyneux initially intended to be an artist, and was diverted into the fashion world when he won a contest sponsored by the famous couturière Lucile, alias Lady Duff Gordon, who subsequently employed him as an illustrator. He travelled the world as her assistant, was conscripted into the army, became a captain and lost his sight in one eye.

Post-Second World War, Molyneux opened his own couture house in London, later opening branches in Cannes and Monte Carlo. In 1950 he was the first dress designer to be honoured with the title of Royal Designer for Industry. Molyneux retired to Jamaica in 1950, but attempted a comeback during the 1960s. Unfortunately, fashion had moved on. His impeccable taste had been elbowed out of the way by outlandish visions of the future. The house of Molyneux, which Balmain described as 'a temple of subdued elegance', could not be resurrected.

MONTANA, Claude

BORN: PARIS, FRANCE, 1949

Noted for his huge shoulder pads, exaggerated proportions and fetishistic tendencies, Claude Montana has survived since the 1960s on a diet of leather and aggressive silhouettes. He has a hard-core client base and his hero, curiously, is Cristobal Balenciaga.

Montana became most famous during the 1980s when his outlandish silhouettes – enormous shoulder spans and tiny waists – perfectly captured the more extreme elements of power-dressing. Later in the decade he experimented with angular silhouettes which did not involve any extraneous padding.

In January 1989 Montana unveiled his first couture collection for Lanvin, telling the *International Herald Tribune*, 'For this collection I feel the need to return to my roots. Things are very pure, structured, aggressive. It is time for that again.' Three years later, with reputed losses of $25 million, Montana was out on his ear. 'We do not wish to continue with Montana for haute couture,' Lanvin's president stated in the *International Herald Tribune*, 'we will definitely not renew our contract with him.' Montana, however, survived, almost immediately launching a lower-priced range called Odyssée, and putting his fashion spat down to experience. 'I brought Montana to them; I brought myself there, all my art, and soul and everything,' he told *W* magazine in his defence. 'It was me. Nobody asked me to be anything but that.'

MORTON, Digby

Born: Dublin, Ireland, 1906
Died: London, England, 1983

'Digby Morton is an Irishman who saw and exploited the beauty of Irish tweeds. He turned them from shy, shapeless garments into immaculately racy, tailored suits,' said *Vogue* in 1946. Morton began designing in 1928, after leaving the Dublin Metropolitan School of Art because he felt that 'it really would take too long to become an architect'.

He moved to London and by 1936 was heading his own company. Morton was one of the most prominent designers of the war years, involved in the design of the government utility collection, and expressing his hobbies as war-time innovation and the preparation of highly seasoned casseroles. He shaped Lachasse into a house with a formidable reputation, and left in 1933 to form his own couture house. His skill with tweed was legendary, as was his ability to tailor. Morton was instrumental in encouraging Scottish weavers to switch from neutral tones to pastels. With an intense dislike of vivid colours, he preferred black, half-tones and pastels, and cited the beauty of Irish tweed as the main reason he switched careers.

OPPOSITE **A 'striking cape-costume' of 1922 by Edward Molyneux: a silk jersey machine-embroidered dress, with a cape held in place by silver plaques.**

RIGHT **'Svelte and structured', the exaggerated proportions of Claude Montana's angelic gown, 1985, is a typical example of the designer's love of powerful clothes with big shoulders.**

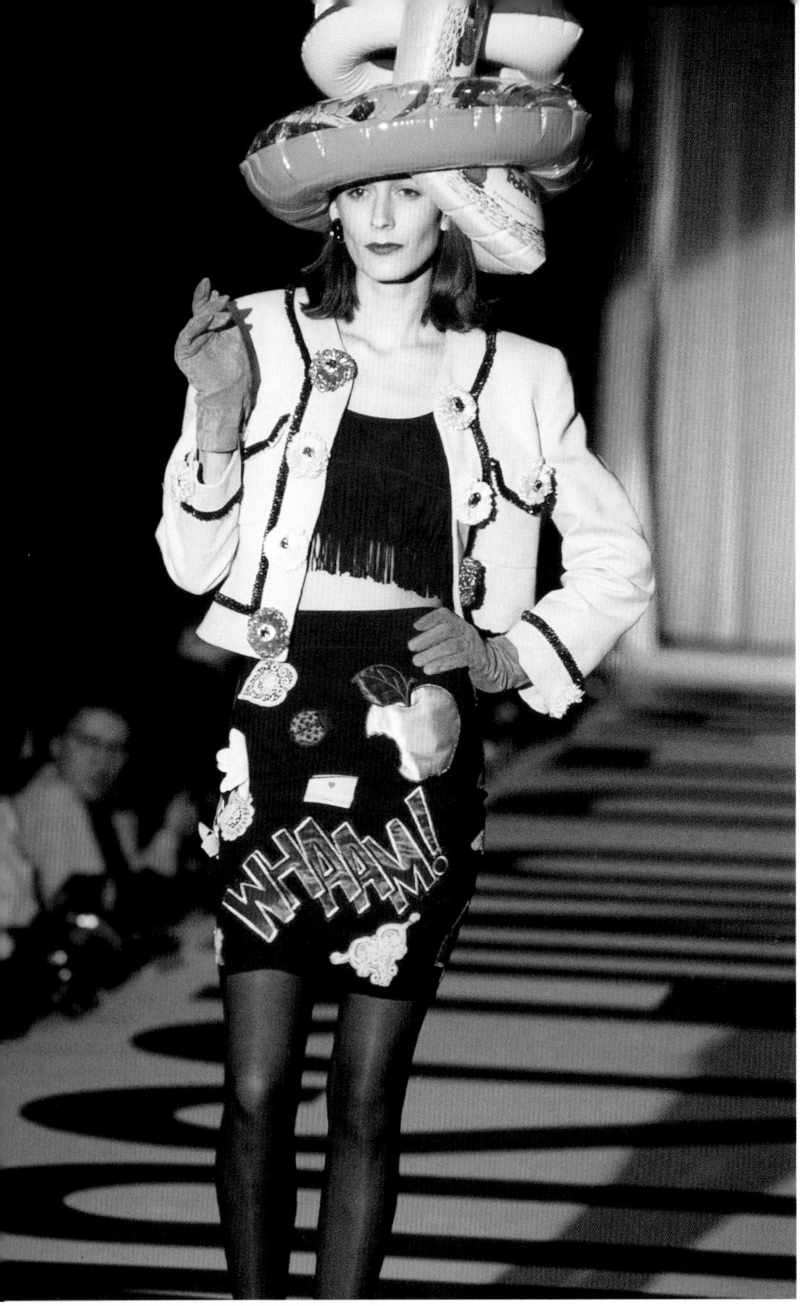
WHAAM!

LEFT Moschino 'breaking the rules' in 1988: colourful, crazy, and deliciously over the top – a skirt that says 'Whaam!' and rubber rings on the head.

OPPOSITE 'Red's hot' in August 1995: Thierry Mugler's curvy, spiky suit with powerful shoulders, sweeping scarves, clever seaming and scorching colour.

MOSCHINO, Franco

BORN: ABBIATEGRASSO, ITALY, 1950
DIED: BRIANZA, ITALY, 1994

A fine artist who fell into fashion by accident, Franco Moschino was the self-styled court jester who sported a crew cut and cocked a snook at convention. His speciality was making a fortune out of irony – he called his labels COUTURE! and CHEAP & CHIC. His belts and bags with 'MOSCHINO' written on them were bestsellers.

Moschino started out as a freelance illustrator, working for, among others, Gianni Versace. In 1969 he progressed to design via an Italian company called Cadette, and launched his own company in 1983. A surrealist at heart, Moschino had more in common with Elsa Schiaparelli than any other designer and his favourite artist, naturally enough, was René Magritte. A typical Moschino statement was to send models down the catwalk wearing carrier bags. In 1993 he staged an exhibition celebrating ten years of fashion called, 'Moschino: X Years of Kaos!'. His favourite ploy was appliqué with a play on words: a jacket with 'Waist of Money' written across it, 'Fashion is Full of Chic' or 'Ready to Where?' Moshino signed his last collection for autumn/winter 1994, which included a waistcoat with the words 'LESS IS MORE' emblazoned across it in black and red. As he described himself, 'Moschino, the Revolutionary, the Prankster, the Provocateur, as always.'

MUGLER, Thierry

BORN: STRASBOURG, FRANCE, 1948

With the original intention of being a ballet dancer, Thierry Mugler leapt through the 1970s and 1980s on a wave of exaggeration, quickly establishing himself as a designer who, whether you love or loathe his work, cannot be ignored. Mugler's inspiration comes from his interpretation of the ultimate femme fatale: Hollywood starlets, vamps, vixens. The woman who would cross the line between divine vision and drag queen. His ideal is Jerry Hall.

Mugler decided to swap a life at the *barre* for a liaison with a pincushion. He discontinued his plans to be a dancer with the Rhine Ballet – 'I couldn't stand to dance the *Swan Lake* one more time,' he told the *Guardian* – and travelled to Paris, working as a window-dresser. After spells living in London and Amsterdam, he returned to Paris and launched his own line in 1974. Throughout the 1970s, 1980s and 1990s, Mugler has kept resolutely to his own course: dispensing a seasonal mix of fetishism, glamour and sexiness, safe in the knowledge that the majority of the world's population would put cleavage over practicality every time.

In 1998 Mugler, who had been taking photographs since 1978, shot a series called 'Sex Couture' for the forty-fifth anniversary issue of *Playboy* magazine. Invariably branded a feminist's nightmare, misogynist fascist and insult to women, Mugler remains completely non-plussed by the criticism. His fragrance, Angel, launched in the mid-1990s, is a bestseller; his clothes sell in droves; his collections always cause a stir. He knows that whichever way the wind blows, the phrase 'sex sells' is a truism for all eternity.

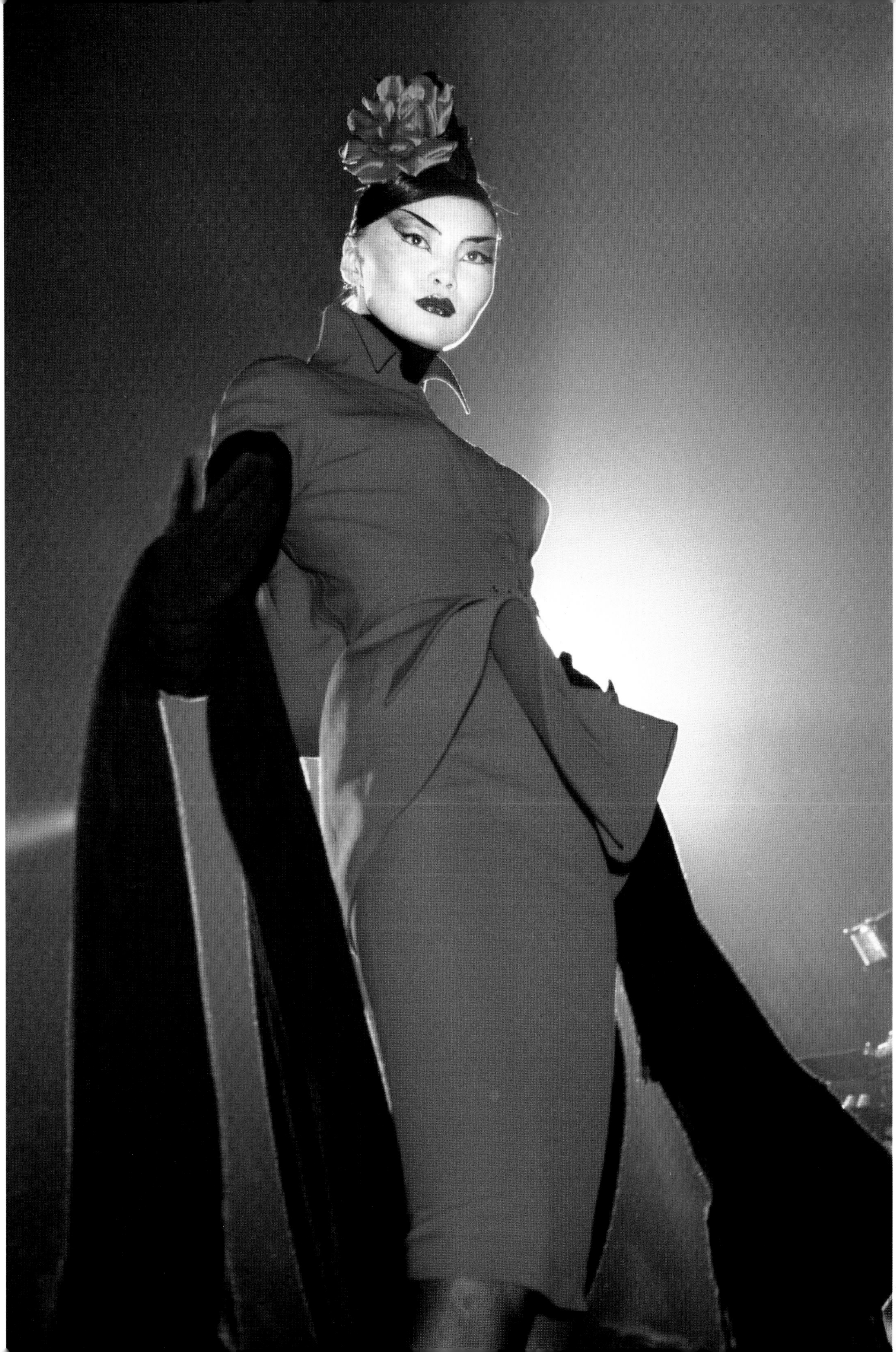

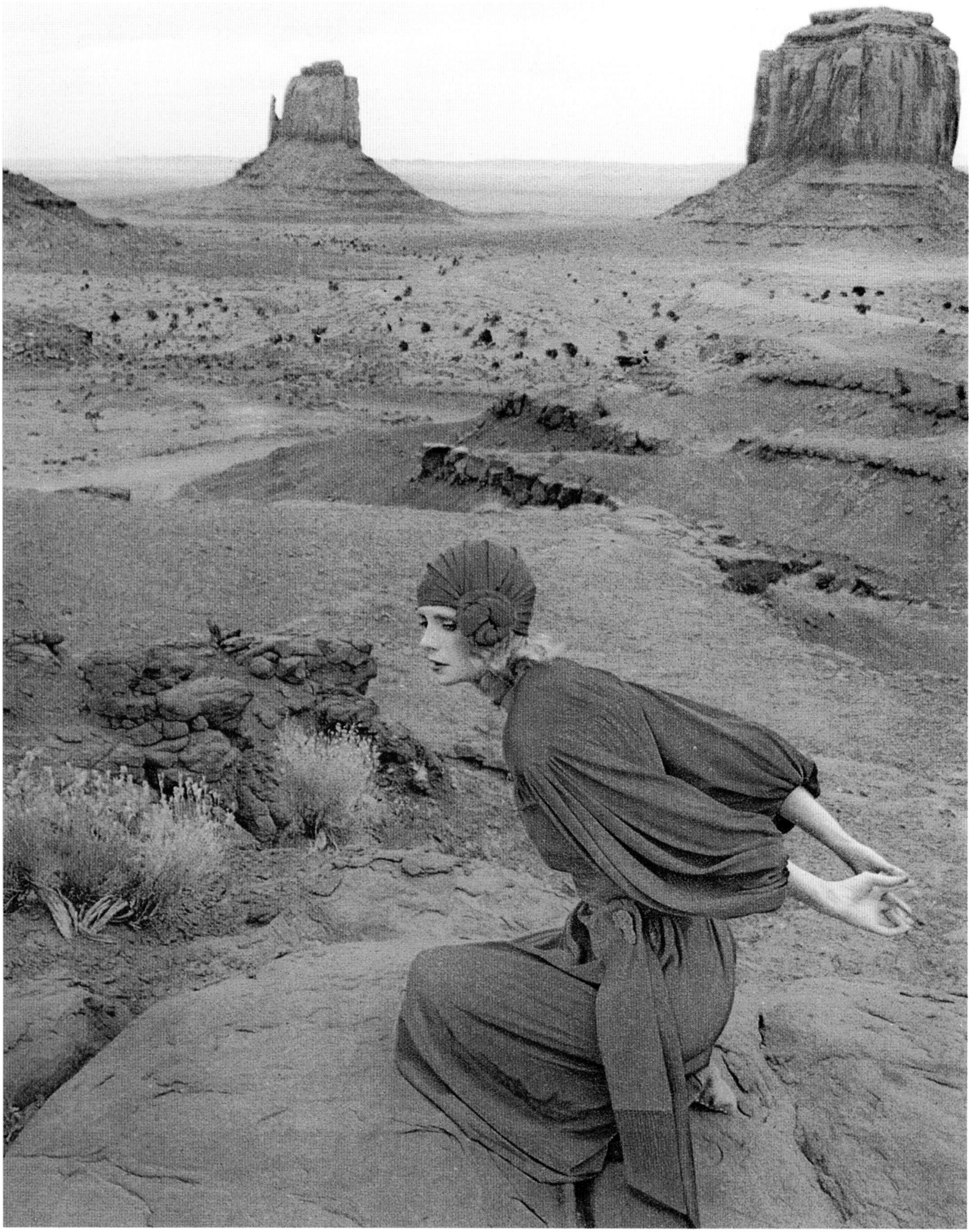

MUIR, Jean

BORN: LONDON, ENGLAND, 1928
DIED: LONDON, ENGLAND, 1995

Jean Muir, the doyenne of dressmaking, had the hands of
a craftswoman, the mind of an engineer and the sensibility of a Scot.
A romantic expressionist with a rod of steel running through, Muir
detested the word 'fashion'. 'Don't call me a fashion designer –
a self-important, pretentious term,' she told *Vogue* in 1978. 'Just
do it importantly.' A perfectionist without compare, in a world of
plummeting standards and disintegrating loyalty, Muir was revered
by her contemporaries and respected by her rivals. She was one
of the few British designers to survive the 1960s.

Muir began her career at Liberty, which she described as her
spiritual home and the art school she never attended. She spent six
years as a designer at Jaeger, before designing under the Jane & Jane
label. By the early 1960s, when others were transfixed by youth, Muir
had formulated her vision – the look that made her famous – jersey,
leather and suede worked into fluid shapes and perfect proportions.

During her illustrious career, Jean Muir accumulated a string of
academic, industrial and international awards: Doctor of Literature
at Newcastle University; a CBE in 1984; an Honorary Citizen of the
City of New Orleans in 1973; Neiman Marcus awards; the Hommage
de la Mode by the Fédération Française du Prêt à Porter Feminine
in 1985; Master of the Faculty of Royal Designers for Industry in
1994. In France they simply called her 'la Reine de la robe'. Muir's
customers included the cream of the artistic and theatrical worlds
– Bridget Riley, Elizabeth Fink, Dame Maggie Smith, Barbra
Streisand, and the most famous ex-house model, Joanna Lumley.
Geraldine Stutz, ex-president of New York department store, Henri
Bendel, described her clothes as 'worth swimming the Channel for'.

Muir was a puritan, an enthusiast, and an original who was always
associated with navy blue but whose colour sense was pure celtic. She
could hold her own in politics, art, business and design; her favourite
subject was the resurgence of the artist-craftsman, a renaissance she
nurtured and predicted a decade before it occurred. A human whirlwind,
with succinct expressions and a wonderful sense of the ridiculous,
Muir was a brilliant one-off. 'She should, *of course*, have been made
a Dame,' said the ex-editor of British *Vogue*, Beatrix Miller, in Muir's
obituary of 1995, echoing the sentiments of admirers everywhere.

OPPOSITE **Muir's signature jersey.
Caught in a breeze in 1971, it
blends into the landscape at
Monument Valley, Arizona, USA.**

RIGHT **Sleek tailoring with
seams precisely positioned for
maximum fit and flare effect:
Muir's perfect suit, 1986.**

INDEX & PICTURE CREDITS

PICTURE CREDITS

The publishers would like to thank the following sources for their kind permission to reproduce the pictures in this book:

t: top, b: bottom, l: left, r: right, tl: top left, tr: top right, bl: bottom left, br: bottom right, bc: bottom centre, bcl: bottom centre left, bcr: bottom centre right.

All images © Vogue, The Condé Nast Publications Ltd.

Antonio 18l
Michel Arnaud 49, 60
David Bailey 10, 15
Cecil Beaton 21, 24, 25,
Christian Berard 41
Bettmann/Corbis (jacket)
Eric Boman 42
Regan Cameron 34, 48
Henry Clarke 13
Patrick Demarchelier 39, 45
Arthur Elgort 23tl, 43
Robert Erdmann 17, 36
Lee Creelman Erickson 46
Michel Haddi 54
Don Honeyman 37tr,
Donna Karan 28
Nick Knight 16, 38
Kim Knott 7,
Eddy Kohli 55
Andrew Lamb 22, 23br, 40, 56, 61
Andrew Macpherson 3, 6
Eamonn J. McCabe 35
Raymond Meier 12
Sheila Metzner 29
David Montgomery 26,
Tom Munro 4, 50, 53
Norman Parkinson 62
Douglas Pollard 52
John Rawlings 47
Lothar Schmid 1, 63
Mario Testino 9, 33
Javier Vallhonrat 27
Tony Viramontes 8
Albert Watson 19c